2004 POETRY

ONCE UPON A RHYME

IMAGINATION FOR
A NEW GENERATION

Poems From Southern England

Edited by Sarah Marshall

 Young**Writers**

First published in Great Britain in 2005 by:
Young Writers
Remus House
Coltsfoot Drive
Peterborough
PE2 9JX
Telephone: 01733 890066
Website: www.youngwriters.co.uk

SB ISBN 1 84460 684 8

Foreword

Young Writers was established in 1991 and has been passionately devoted to the promotion of reading and writing in children and young adults ever since. The quest continues today. Young Writers remains as committed to engendering the fostering of burgeoning poetic and literary talent as ever.

This year's Young Writers competition has proven as vibrant and dynamic as ever and we are delighted to present a showcase of the best poetry from across the UK. Each poem has been carefully selected from a wealth of *Once Upon A Rhyme* entries before ultimately being published in this, our twelfth primary school poetry series.

Once again, we have been supremely impressed by the overall high quality of the entries we have received. The imagination, energy and creativity which has gone into each young writer's entry made choosing the best poems a challenging and often difficult but ultimately hugely rewarding task - the general high standard of the work submitted amply vindicating this opportunity to bring their poetry to a larger appreciative audience.

We sincerely hope you are pleased with our final selection and that you will enjoy *Once Upon A Rhyme Poems From Southern England* for many years to come.

Contents

Aaron Poole (12)   1
Alex Brown (13)   2

Bordon Junior School, Bordon
Drew Munn (10)   3

Branksome Heath Middle School, Poole
Kimberly Jayne Pringle (10)   4
Victoria Stubbs (10)   5
Maisie Havelock-Smith (11)   6
Chloe Holness (10)   6
Laura West (11)   7
Joseph Garrett (10)   8

Buckland Newton CE Primary School, Dorchester
Lauren Daniel (10)   8
Tom Lawday (10)   9
Amelia Tavenner (10)   9
Daniel Calcott (10)   10
James J Olley (10)   10
David Tuke (10)   11
Abigail House (10)   11
Joseph Slack (10)   12
Luke Gain (10)   13
Flora Brown (10)   14
Ricky Rowland (10)   15
Caitlin Palmer (10)   16
Yasmin Froud (10)   17
Georgina Spinney (10)   18
Rosie Foot (10)   19
Zoe Pollard (10)   20

Conifers School, Midhurst
Matilda Corfield (10)   20
Alexandra Suter (11)   21
Charlotte Amelia Homan (9)   21
Tara Ogilvy (10)   22
Nairne Fraser (9)   22

Joanna Charlotte Carey (9)   23
Katie Oldworth (10)   23
Lily Venables Kyrke (10)   24
Francesca Suter (9)   24
Gemma Clarke (10)   25
Purdie Oldworth (9)   25
Anja-Grace Schulp (10)   26
Katherine Oliver (8)   26
Ellie Lusona-Sears (11)   27
Dana Kamour (8)   27
Maddy Sanders (10)   28
Tabitha Taylor (9)   29

Fletching CE Primary School, Fletching

Lauren Hayes (11)   29
Grace Minney (8)   30
Hayleigh Horscroft (11)   30
Georgina Lafbery (10)   31
Philippa Grace Penfold (10)   32
Anneli Robinson (10)   33
Isabella Holopov (9)   34
Alex Cove (9)   34
Ben Arnold (9)   35
Chantelle Evangline Cove (11)   35
Magenta Kemp (9)   36
Ben Sumpter (8)   36
Laura Oxley (9)   37
Sarah White (9)   38
Chloe Rowlinson (8)   39
Cassie Galpin (10)   40
Laura Cowling (8)   41

Great Ballard School, Eartham

Amy Furlong (10)   41
Jessica Simmonds (10)   42
Amelia Pickles (10)   43
Clara Butterworth (10)   44
Ysabelle Shopland (10)   44
Anne Cole (10)   45
Oliver Coombe-Tennant (10)   45
Hayley Mackay (10)   46

Billy Darby (11)   46
Emma Ponsford (8)   46
Elisa Castro (10)   47
Isla Paterson (8)   47
Madeleine Leaver (8)   48
Harriet Simmonds (8)   48
Matilda Pickles   49
Jake Reed (8)   49
Hannah Mason (10)   50

Heathfield Junior School, Sholing
Bradley Coole (10)   50
Joel Whitfield (10)   51
Marie Emily Dunleavy (10)   51
Pamala Williams (10)   52
Daniel Brooks (10)   52
Rhys Sullivan (11)   52
Ryan Lakey (10)   53
Amanda Phillips (11)   53
Alexandra Katie Hill (10)   54
Lennie J Read (10)   54
Matthew Burt (10)   54
Bethany Thomson (10)   55
Brandon Dawson (10)   55
Ashleigh Houghton (10)   55
Conor Whyte (10)   56
Thomas Williams (10)   56
Michael Watts (10)   57
Lauren Hobbs (10)   57
Bethany Doyle (10)   58

Hordle Walhampton School, Walhampton
George Farrar   58
Michael Truell (11)   59
Soraya Allen (12)   59
Lucy Ogilvie   60
Jamie Gossage (11)   61
Charlie Skinner (12)   61
Laura Wiltshire (11)   62
Marco Mills (12)   62
Lubinda Lishomwa (8)   63

Ben Willis (12)   63
Emily Orford (8)   63
Bree Roberts (8)   64
Tara Clapham (8)   64
Ben Crane (9)   64
Humphrey Bonsor (9)   65
Shane Devlin (11)   65
Hannah Lees (8)   66
Guy Wilkinson (8)   66
Georgina Lewis (8)   66
Marina McWhirter (8)   67
Joshua Rehel (8)   67
James Dare (10)   68
Rachel Lee (8)   68
Harry Vokins (8)   69
Orlando Kary (8)   69
Arabella Gamble (11)   70
Charlie Banks (10)   70
Isabella Wallrock (8)   71

Oakfield Primary School, Totton
Harry Tatner (10)   72

Oakwood School, Oakwood
Hattie Rawlins (8)   72
Toby Allison (8)   73
Alexander Russell (8)   73
Katie Sharp (9)   74
Faith Withinshaw (8)   74
Natasha Morgan (9)   75
Georgiana Osborn (8)   75
Emily Hutchin (8)   76
Dominic Wood (9)   76
Ellen Lavender (8)   77
George Cunningham (8)   77
Brontë Graham (9)   78
Louisa Filary (9)   78
Olivia Sumner (9)   78
Jack Sheeran (9)   79
Guy Mansell (9)   79
Elli Lytton (9)   79

Robbie Holden (9)	80
George Hamilton-Green (9)	80
Alec Walker (8)	81
Laura Greenfield (8)	81
Harriet Field (9)	82
Harry Johnson (8)	82
Innes Hopkins (8)	83
Victoire Michel (9)	83
Josh Brooke-Jones	84
Daisy Strange (9)	84
Travis Torode (9)	84
Henry Foster (9)	85
Jamie Munro (9)	85

Ocklynge County Junior School, Eastbourne

Charlotte Higby (10)	85
Kyle Whittlesey (9)	86
Kitty Nielsen (9)	86
Hollie Wilkins (9)	86
Tom Pashley (9)	87
Chris Maskill (9)	87
Jessica Woodrow (9)	87
Gary Fry (9)	88
Jason Taylor (11)	88
Leah Kiely (9)	88
Curtis Mays (10)	89
Michelle Turner (9)	89
David Purton (10)	90
Anna-Marie Wright (10)	90
Roxy Knights (11)	91
William McIntyre (10)	91
Lucy Gray (10)	92
Rachael Reed (10)	92
Jessica Clarke (10)	93
Jamie Sivers (10)	93
Hannah Barnato-Ludbrook (10)	94
Charlotte White (10)	94
Nathan Visick (10)	95
Matthew Stace (10)	95
Nicole Hoddinott (10)	96
Emma Thursfield (10)	96

Lily Stoneley (10)	97
Glen Morgan (10)	97
Jasmine Curtis-McFetters (11)	98
Charlie Pearson (10)	98
Jacob Adlam (10)	98
Abigail Lain (10)	99
Alicia Pettit (10)	99
Thomas Wardale (10)	100
Roya Arjomand (10)	100
Jack Williams (10)	101
Matthew Khan (10)	101
Courtney Dyer (10)	102
Lewis Smith (10)	102

Park Gate Primary School, Southampton

Anastasia Taylor (7)	103

Parkland J&I School, Eastbourne

David Dumbleton (10)	103
Laura Grant (10)	104
Alex Haywood (11)	104
Joshua Rank (10)	105
Timothy Carr (10)	106
Elliott Field (10)	106
Kelsey McCann (10)	107
Natasha Cameron (10)	107
Declan Gee (10)	108
Jessica Capon (9)	108
Victoria Baldwin (10)	109
Natalie Healey & Tamar Hawkins (10)	109
Michael Shefford (10)	110
Sophie Wormald (10)	110
Alistair Home (10)	111
Stephanie Hellier (11)	111
Megan Prangnell Montieth (10)	112
Ellen Mathias-Bevan (10)	112
Lloyd Thursfield (10)	113
Christopher Blackman (10)	113
Pia Jackson (10)	114
Beth Adams (10)	115
Dan Waters (10)	116

Peter Gladwin Primary School, Portslade

Chloe Ralphs (10)	116
Timmy Dunkerton (11)	117
Ione Gamble (10)	117
Aaron Brace (11)	118
Matthew Grant (10)	118
Paige Wickens (10)	119
Bryony Reynolds (10)	119
George Dunkerton (11)	120
Isi Fink (10)	120
Darcey Clark (10)	121
Sam Ralphs (10)	121
Sam Talbot (10)	122
Daniel Hart (11)	122
Rebekah Strong (10)	123
Sarah Green (10)	123
Katie Lillywhite (10)	124
Ben Ffitch (10)	125
Stefen Chapman (10)	126
Georgia Cronin (10)	127

Portfield Community Primary School, Chichester

Claudia Cole (10)	127
Shanice Wilson (10)	128
Ryan Ellis (11)	128
Dominic Mortimer (10)	129
Rachael Ambler (10)	130

Rotherfield Primary School, Crowborough

Esther Akehurst (6)	130
Oliver Pilbeam (8)	131
Mirran Harper (7)	131
Sam Osborne (7)	132
Harry Chittenden (6)	132
Holly Jenkins (6)	133
James Miller (7)	133
Lucy Evans (7)	134
Brooke Steadman (6)	134
Hannah Russell (8)	135
Katy Jackson (7)	135
Denver Weller-Tomsett (7)	136

Arthur William Walker (7)	136
Olivia Charles (7)	137
Robert Allison (7)	137
Sophie-Rose McDonagh (7)	138
Max Bates (7)	138
Amy Dodd (7)	139
Fergus Wilson (7)	139
Nathan Dewhurst (6)	140
Sophie Gray (7)	140
Jake Tibbutt (8)	141

St Giles CE Primary School, Horsted Keynes
Laura Willis (10)	142

St Margaret's CE Primary School, Ditchling
Alfie Goldsmith (10)	143
George Waring (10)	143
Georgina Marshall (9)	144
Scarlett Pickup (10)	144
Nicola Bowman (9)	145
Luke Buckman (8)	145
Ben Rudling (10)	146
Rebecca Bennis (9)	146
Hannah Skinner & George Greenstreet (10)	147
Jamie Beveridge (9)	147
Sam Sanders (10)	148

St Mark's CE Primary School, Hadlow Down
Alex Blowey (9)	148
Katie Lee (9)	148
Carys Coleman (10)	149
Stefan Godfrey (9)	149
Helen Michaelson-Yeates (9)	150
Declan Dunkley (9)	150
Amy-Lee Stiller (9)	151
Tilly Sherwood (10)	151
Christie McMenamin (10)	151
Daniel Hansell (8)	152
Jesse Coleman (8)	152
Claudia Vince (9)	152
Elizabeth Durant (10)	153

St Richard's RC School, Chichester

Alicia White (9)	153
Lucy Brookes (9)	154
Tom Hurst (9)	154
Isaac Salt (9)	155
Tessa Newman (9)	155
Caterina Atkinson (9)	156
Melissa Sykes (9)	156
Harry Henshaw (9)	157
Harry Martin (10)	157
Roisin McNally (10)	158

St Thomas More's Catholic Primary School, Havant

Claudia Tyler (10)	159

Southwater Junior School, Horsham

Aimee Rogers (10)	160
Olivia Watkinson (10)	160
Louisa Clark (10)	161
William Nash (10)	161
Anja Dolphin (11)	162
Adam Hockley (10)	162
Jack Wilcox (11)	163
Charlotte Cowlin (11)	163
Isabelle Allison (10)	164
Chloe Miles (9)	164
Jennifer Powell (10)	165
Drew Taylor (10)	166

Tollgate Community Junior School, Eastbourne

Emily Meeks (7)	166
Samantha Steer (10)	167
Bayan Fenwick (10)	167
Ella Garraway (8)	168
Bronwyn Ryan (7)	168
Emily Bailey (10)	169
Amy Garnell (7)	170
Olivia Groves (7)	170
Laura Cardin (7)	171
Lydia Crossey (8)	171
Liam Mason (10)	171

Western Road Community Primary School, Lewes

Rachel Limage (9)	172
Beth Arscott (9)	172
Tamara Carruthers-Cole (9)	173
Will Anthony (9)	173
Yoli Ward-Streeter (9)	174
JJ Frizell (9)	174
Ayisha Ascioglu (9)	174
Beth Crouch (9)	175
Louise Astbury (9)	175
Alice Chapman (9)	176
Luke Tomsett (9)	176
Xanthe Wharton (9)	177
Kaleem Luthra (9)	177
Noah Preston (10)	178
Megan Edwards (9)	178
Zoë Vernon (8)	179
Laura Keenan-Hall (9)	179
Bryony Hockin (10)	180
Madeleine Lewis (10)	180
Jack Arscott (11)	181
Eddie Lansley (7)	181
Rupert Flowers (9)	181
Vita Bowman (10)	182
Rosie Chapman (10)	182
Thomas Morrish (10)	183
Nikolas Long (10)	183

Winton Primary School, Bournemouth

Isabel Lloyd (10)	184
Andrew Lavender (11)	184
Emily Riddiough (10)	185
Valerija Lvova (10)	185
Daniel Burden (10)	186
Jade Atkinson & Tayler Smith (10)	186
Tegen Jones (11)	187
Fern Whiting (10)	187
Lisa Mills (10)	188
Georgia Wallen (10)	189
Charles Rodriguez (10)	190
Rachel Drewitt (11)	191

Emily Head (10)	192
Simon Barton (10)	193
Beth Lamb (10)	194
Jacob West (11)	195
Mica Cornell (10)	196
Nadia Ghazal (10)	197
Charlotte Caesar (10)	198

Wyke Regis Junior School, Weymouth

Nathan James (10)	198
Joe Allen (10)	199
Sophie King (11)	199
Edward Beauchamp (10)	200
George Dukes (10)	200
Joshua Jenkins (10)	201
David Bain (10)	201
Mica Satchell (10)	202
Robyn Nixon (10)	202
James Pearson (10)	203
Megan Arnold (10)	203
Stacey Bray (10)	204
Christopher Griffiths (10)	204
Louise Daynes (10)	205
Andrew Whyte (10)	205
Evan Feltham (10)	206
Sophie Hardy (10)	206
Aarynn Carter (10)	207
Amber Downing (10)	207
Gemma McNie (11)	208

The Poems

Jamaica

Reggae music fills the air
In Jamaica the spirit is there.

They have dreadlocks in their hair
Jamaican music fills the air.

Jamaica, Jamaica, dreadlock rastas!
Jamaica, Jamaica, dreadlock masters!

Hot sun setting in the Caribbean
Beautiful scenery is what we're seeing.

Luscious cool blue and green seas
Filled with colourful fishes.

Tropical coconuts on the trees
Swaying gently in the breeze.

Jamaica's blessed with year-round sun
And a laid-back attitude in everyone.

In Jamaica the job is done
But - they always do it with a bit of fun.

Aaron Poole (12)

Different Faces

Everyone's different, including *me!*
Look in our class and you will see.

The Italian kid,
The Spanish kid,

The one that's my *size.*

The *coloured* kid,
The *quiet* kid,
The one with *beautiful eyes.*

The *loud* kid,
The *brainy* kid,
The one who runs a mile.

The *good* kid,
The *naughty* kid,
The one with the great smile.

Everyone's different, including me,
Everyone's equal and that's how it should be!

Alex Brown (13)

Changing World

The world is changing ev'ry day,
Even though you don't always see it,
From fire to electric,
From stone to brick,
The world changes.
From records to CDs,
From wagons to cars,
The world changes.
From love to greed,
From help to self-satisfaction,
Don't let it happen,
Technology is dangerous,
But can be useful in good hands.
As the world develops, it also dies,
Fish and plants are taken for granted,
But for them, it's no game,
It's a fight,
A fight for life.
Don't kill the world.

Drew Munn (10)
Bordon Junior School, Bordon

Monsters Under My Bed

The monsters under my bed
have all got special names
the green one is called Fred
and the yellow one is James.

The purple one is Lily
she's got a big, blue spot
she can be rather silly
but of course so can Dot.

Glen is friends with Ben
Lily likes James a lot
the oldest one is ten
and everyone knows it's Dot.

James is such a pain
he annoys the boys
the blame is put on Shane
cos he breaks all the toys.

My friends say I lie
they say I've got a big bed
I'll know it's true until I die
that they're just in my head!

Kimberly Jayne Pringle (10)
Branksome Heath Middle School, Poole

The Castle Of No Return

The castle's walls are blood-red
With rust from water pounding down
From the shadowy skies.

Windows as black as a wolf's mouth
And an oak door as gigantic
As the sky itself.

Based on a hill towering over the village
That lifts the castle
Up to the heavens.

The moon illuminates
The skeletons of a dead orchard
And not a sound is heard from within.

The wind whistles in-between the turrets
Decorated with horrifying faces
Of mythical beasts.

Not a soul goes in there
Not a soul comes out
Behold the many mysteries of this haunted house.

Victoria Stubbs (10)
Branksome Heath Middle School, Poole

The Railway Race

A slamming of doors,
A swishing of locks
And he's off!

Whizzing down the track,
As if he'll never stop.

Hurtling round the corner,
Just like a speeding car.

The creaking of brakes,
A screaming of wheels
And yes, he's made it,
He's finished and stopped!

Maisie Havelock-Smith (11)
Branksome Heath Middle School, Poole

Summer's Decoration

A green blanket is laid on the bare ground
My winter clothes, I take off
I start to put on my pink and green jewellery
Then I put on my green and different-shaped clothes
I am not alone, for I have creatures with me.

I unfold my arms so that more birds can join me
Woodlice and other bugs live in and by my feet
Squirrels bury their nuts under my toes
I have grown taller and have new skin
Birds pick up my old skin and use it for their nests.

In the warm night I sway happily to and fro
Foxes come and dig by my lower hands.

Chloe Holness (10)
Branksome Heath Middle School, Poole

Telling Tales

Miss, Miss,
I don't want to sit next to Michael Jane,
He picks his nose again and again,
I don't like those trousers he wears
And he seems to have grown lots of new hairs.

Miss, Miss,
I don't want to sit here,
The noise of the classroom is right in my ear,
The teacher's telling people what to do,
Can't I please go to the loo?
I'm fed up with all this fuss,
I'd rather sit next to my worst friend, Gus.

Go on then, sit next to him,
But then you'll be away from Jim.

Oh no, I'd rather sit next to Michael Jane,
Oh no, not this again!

Please, please, *please* just settle down
And please Maria, take off that gown,
You all know you are driving me insane,
I'm sure my poor head aches again.

Please Miss, can I move place,
I promise I'll work at a quicker pace.

I've got a good idea,
Why don't you just move classroom!

Laura West (11)
Branksome Heath Middle School, Poole

It's Summer

It's getting really hot
put away your warm clothes, get out all your cool ones
the beaches flood with people
small, tall, round and large.

It's getting really hot
the golden sun shines down from above
it's getting really fun now for everyone
small, tall, round and large.

It's getting really hot
as warm as a raging fire
but it is still fun for everyone
small, tall, round and large.

But now it turns to winter
it's getting really chilly
the beaches are empty and cold
while everyone sits by the fire enjoying a good book.

Joseph Garrett (10)
Branksome Heath Middle School, Poole

Tame Versus Wild

In the warm house, in front of the fire,
A tired fox lays stretched out, warming itself,
While the cat is outside, shivering in the dark coldness,
Watching for her prey, what will it be tonight?

The moon shimmers, fully glowing in the dark,
A mouse howls, echoingly,
Up to the starry night,
While the wolf in his hole,
        nibbles delightedly on a piece of fresh cheese.

A panther lies down on the comfortable bed,
Sleeping against his owner, snuggling into him tight,
While outside in the jungle, a crafty dog prowls cautiously,
Sneaking up on a helpless bird, who has just been born.

Lauren Daniel (10)
Buckland Newton CE Primary School, Dorchester

A Recipe For An Exciting Night In Front Of The Telly

First of all, get a Ready Steady Cook's bowl,
Then add two screaming ambulances from Casualty,
Whisk in half-a-pint of Guinness from Lou's pub,
Mix in Ann Robinson's glasses,
Knead in Chief Wiggum's half-eaten doughnut,
Rub in Pat's earrings until creamy,
Blend in a crisp million pound cheque from Chris Tarrant,
Combine the mixture with Indiana Jones' whip,
Mix in Jazz's cool groovy hat,
Add Bradley's shining trainers to make it reach for the stars,
Incorporate three eggs from Mr Tweedy's chicken farm,
Chop one of Michael Schumacher's jet-black tyres into small pieces,
Next, mix in James Bond's gun,
Finally, pre-heat your sofa to 160-180°C,
Grease your baking tin and pour in the mouth-watering mixture,
Cook it for two hours on your sofa.

Tom Lawday (10)
Buckland Newton CE Primary School, Dorchester

The Moon

The sun fades and the moon journeys out,
Looking at the ant-like people below.
It shines,
Beaming as resplendent as the stars beside him.
But what does he do, sitting by himself?
Perhaps he talks to the chatty stars all night long?
Of course not,
He sits on his comfy rocking chair,
With some deepest black and rich gold paint,
Painting the starry sky, lighting up the darkness all around.

Amelia Tavenner (10)
Buckland Newton CE Primary School, Dorchester

Recipe For Dads

I'm going to cook up a recipe,
Which one shall I do?
There's a lot to complete,
I think I'll do dads,
They're the easiest to achieve.

Hmm . . . what's first?
Ah, a teaspoon of sugar and spice,
Mixed up with ten hours of work,
Blended with half an hour of eating,
Add fifteen minutes of washing-up,
Plus three hours of TV.
The final ingredient is ten hours of sleep on a comfy chair,
Mix it up with a wooden spoon,
Put it in the oven for one hour,
Then pour it on the sofa
And in one minute, you'll have a new dad!

Daniel Calcott (10)
Buckland Newton CE Primary School, Dorchester

Dog Recipe

I want a big, fluffy dog,
So I'll make one.
Now, I'll need:
Four springs, two beads,
Anger of a teacher,
Strong fur coat and black food colouring.
A hangman's noose and a flask of deep red wine.
Now to put in four springs and the fur coat and stir.
Now put in the rest.
At last, here's a dog.
Oops! I forgot the strings
As the dog collapses.

James J Olley (10)
Buckland Newton CE Primary School, Dorchester

What Am I?

I'm like a dark lord from space,
Revving the powerful engine,
As I goes up the hill's back.
I load the trailer like a crane
And haul it back to the barn.
The building like a monumental arch,
Towering over the disk-like bales,
Unloading the trailer with my colossal loader.
Summertime is over, winter has begun.

Chopping straw, working hard,
Feeding the cows with juicy silage,
Mixing wheat and minerals, adding sticky molasses.
The cows have eaten, time for milking.
Scraping up the giant yards ready for later.
I like diesel and oil, I have a lot of lights.

What am I?

David Tuke (10)
Buckland Newton CE Primary School, Dorchester

My Cat

I've got a tabby cat
Named Matt,
He is very fat,
He sleeps on a gigantic mat.

For breakfast he hunts,
For a big, juicy bat,
For tea he eats a rat,
He even has a shrew for lunch,
He'll eat anything, my cat Matt.

Even a dog is on the menu tonight,
With milk and a big, curly straw,
A big fish with a fat rabbit,
When he came home, he couldn't fit through the cat flap,
Poor cat, he can't have supper anymore.

Abigail House (10)
Buckland Newton CE Primary School, Dorchester

School Pie!

'I'm making a school pie today!' said Jill,
'So I'd better follow the instructions carefully . . .'

First, get your light, fluffy pastry
And carefully place it into a bowl.
Then add:

100 grams of stampeding children, running down the corridor,
300 grams of arithmetic, English and science,
Two tablespoons of lectures by the head teacher,
A pinch of detention and a dollop of homework,
Then, just for flavour, sprinkle on some of the head teacher's hair
(The same stuff he pulled out from the lecture.)

Stir for about four minutes, until the class cause mayhem!
Place in the oven, until little monsters start popping out of the top.
If you want to save the pie, place clingfilm around the dessert and bowl
And store in a cool, dry area.

'Funny recipe, but it tastes great!'

The next day at school came,
But when Jill got there, there was no stampede,
No arithmetic, English or science
And the head teacher had a very different haircut!

Joseph Slack (10)
Buckland Newton CE Primary School, Dorchester

Recipe For Maths

I am going to choose maths for my recipe.
OK lets get all the ingredients.
We need one teaspoon of subtraction, ten ounces of partitioning.
Eighteen ounces of *bidmas.*
One hundred and one ounces of multiplication
And two teaspoons of division.
Last of all, five ounces of maths.

Now, to put them together.
First of all, we need to put the ingredients in order.
Next, put the two teaspoons of division in.
Oh no! I forgot the tools.
OK, I need one bowl, knife, cooker and a whisk.

Now I can go back to the two teaspoons of division.
Now, put the two teaspoons in the bowl.
Then whisk the two teaspoons of the division.
Then pour the eighteen ounces of *bidmas.*
Put your hands in and press.
When you have finished that, add the five ounces of maths.
After that, add one hundred and one ounces of multiplication.

Now add one teaspoon of subtraction
And then sprinkle the ten ounces of partitioning.
After you have done that, put it in the oven for forty minutes.
When the cooker goes *tick*, take the recipe out.
After that, cut it in half and roll it all out.
Then you will have a maths book.

Luke Gain (10)
Buckland Newton CE Primary School, Dorchester

Midnight Winter Poem

In the middle of the night,
The black cat was prancing in the winter winds,
As the creature was leaping from lawn to lawn,
He shivered to the beat of his thumping heart.

Every single time he paused in a garden,
His beady little eyes flickered from place to place,
Seeking for somewhere to sit, somewhere to lie,
Somewhere to curl up and fall to sleep.

The animal ran to the stone brick house, number 1,
When he had reached the pure white door of the house,
He suddenly realised that every other door in the village was black,
But this door was white, covered in snow.

The black beast was just about to scamper away,
When all the snow on the door slid down.
Like custard in a jug and fell on the cat.
Like millions of marshmallows falling into a black sea.

He leapt out of the snow like a cannon ball,
Then he froze and pricked his ears up,
He had heard the creak of his master's front door,
He sprinted as fast as a cheetah into the child's arms.

Flora Brown (10)
Buckland Newton CE Primary School, Dorchester

It Wasn't Me

I don't know why the cat's all tied up,
Or who smashed the window with a cup.
I didn't turn the cooker to maximum heat,
Or bring in dirty, muddy feet.
It wasn't me, it was him!

Who did chuck food at the mat,
Or ripped and tore Grandma's hat?
Who tampered with the telly wire,
Or who broke the deep fat fryer?
It wasn't me, it was him!

Maybe it was Dad who kicked the chair,
Or perhaps he threw the cup down the stairs?
Maybe it was him Mum, you should know
Who stood on Grandpa's toe?
It wasn't me, it was him!

Are you sure it's me?
It's plainly him, can't you see?
I've been sat here all the time,
He has committed all the crime.

Ricky Rowland (10)
Buckland Newton CE Primary School, Dorchester

The Winter Beasts

The wind whispers bleakly,
Dancing through the wilderness of winter,
For it is that time of the season,
When the weather rouses the lonely, imprisoned beasts.

It is the heart of winter,
The snow walks silently down to produce a savage wolf,
Leaves swirl around in a blizzard to form a fearsome lion,
The rain and hailstones crash down on the earth to construct
                                        a riled bear,
Furthermore, an air dragon sails menacingly up in the sky,
But its roaring fire turns into gigantic frozen icicles.

Soon the uncivilised devils will be concealed for yet another year,
The taught snow-wolf's brittle coat withstands the wild weather,
While he scatters the vivid snow over the ashamed tree's crisp leaves,
The brave-hearted lion and ragged bear,
Race between the people's dead gardens,
Making leaves soar up into the tense sky,
Where the scaly dragon lies on the fluffy white clouds,
Trying to warm his icicle covered flames.

It will soon be spring,
When the baby animals awaken,
But the untamed beasts have gone,
Dissolved and liquefied,
They will reappear once again,
The fiends that devour the land,
The repulsive creatures that survive
The groggy, chilly, cold conditions,
The winter beasts.

Caitlin Palmer (10)
Buckland Newton CE Primary School, Dorchester

Recipe For Winter

How to make a stormy winter with a snowy top.
You will need:
5oz of vicious, blustery, strong wind
20oz of hailstones from the south
10oz of dangerous, non-stop rain
8oz of thumping thunder and lashing lightning
10oz of freezing snow from Finland
3oz of a strong, blustery day
1oz of hot chocolate powder to warm you up.

How to make it:
Sieve 5oz of blustery, strong wind into a large bowl
Add 20oz of hailstones from the south
Add the rain
Mix everything together
And then add all of the delicious thunder and lightning
Add half a blustery day, mix it all together
Now include the rest of the blustery day
Next, get a whisk and mix it all up
It may look like a lot of bubbles,
But it will turn out all right.
You now need to sieve the 10oz of snow
And 1oz of chocolate powder, add that on top
And put outside to cook for 10 minutes.
Step outside and be prepared to be blown away!

Yasmin Froud (10)
Buckland Newton CE Primary School, Dorchester

Recipe For Summer

My recipe for a perfect summer:

5oz of the hot beach in Spain
6oz of freezing water fight
3oz of delicious BBQ food
10oz of the scintillating sun
8oz of fantastic holiday fun
6oz of relaxing laziness
5oz of active sports.

Chop the BBQ food into small cubes
Mix in with 3oz of the water fights
Whisk together until it has turned mushy
Separately mix the holiday fun and the rest of the water fight
Until light and fluffy
Put in the fridge for 15 minutes.

Combine the beach in Spain and laziness
With BBQ food and water fights
Turn on the oven to 40° with no clouds
Add the active sports and the scintillating sun
To the main bowl and put in everything else
Knead for 5 minutes
Place the mixture in a bucket
Put it in the oven for the summer.

In the winter, it will remind you
Of your magnificent, lazy summer!

Georgina Spinney (10)
Buckland Newton CE Primary School, Dorchester

Creation

The trees quietly whispered to each other,
Why me?
Thought the animal as it scurried out of its dwelling,
Little home.
God silently started
Making a new life
Welcoming to His breathtaking kingdom.
Then suddenly, He lowered His pale blue eyes
And said, 'My kingdom will now be named *the world!'*

The grass swayed violently
While the sea proudly bowed to the forceful master.
Above all, slowly the big, orange celestial sphere
Made its move into the fluffy clouds
That danced like prancing spring lambs.
Eventually, the first day of the world was over,
The first two humans of the planet, stood
Dancing under the starry night sky,
While the master we worship,
Sat in the feathery-cotton clouds,
Pondering His empire below.

Rosie Foot (10)
Buckland Newton CE Primary School, Dorchester

The Black Figure

A black figure galloping through the waking fields,
Going as fast as a blink of an eye,
Swishing and throwing her tail like a windmill,
Her mane flying everywhere,
She speeds across the grassy earth.

Moving quickly through the meadows,
She barely damages the turf.
You hear the sound under the ground
As she speedily travels the surface,
Zooming through the air, she covers the land.

Impressing the wind around her,
She imagines she's in a race.
Discovering how swift she can go,
She stops . . . !
Rolls on the dewy grass,
Gets up and gallops towards the rising sun.

Zoe Pollard (10)
Buckland Newton CE Primary School, Dorchester

My Granny!

My granny was a superstar
She lived in a house with two dogs and a car!

She was brilliant and kind
Loving and caring and made delicious puddings
Just for sharing!

Whenever Granny came to stay
She would bring a cake
Probably made that day.

She loved to make me scones with jam
And very occasionally, some hot roast lamb!

Matilda Corfield (10)
Conifers School, Midhurst

My Granny Was Once A Rock Star

My granny was once a rock star
She used to drive round in a really cool car!

She would travel all over the world
And never, ever get tired or old.
She would sing anywhere and everywhere
Even in France around Val D'Isere.

When she went to Thailand,
She decided to form her own rock band!
Later, when she went to France
She made up a really cool dance!

She liked to sing out loud,
After her songs, she always bowed!
When she was on her way back,
She wrote a song about the colour black.

My granny was the best rock star ever
And to this day, she still wears leather!

Alexandra Suter (11)
Conifers School, Midhurst

Teatime Order

An egg, some flour and plenty of milk,
Mix it all up like liquid silk,
Lots of air and sugar please,
No salt or pepper - I don't want to sneeze.

Make sure the pan is very hot,
Put in the oil, a great big blot,
Toss it and turn it and don't let it stick
And make it thin, it's mushy thick.

Once on the plate, more sugar please,
Sprinkle it over with plenty of ease,
Then add the juice of a tasty lemon,
Eat it all up - I'm in heaven!

Charlotte Amelia Homan (9)
Conifers School, Midhurst

The Apple Tree

There's an apple tree in my garden,
Which is very tall and green.
It has so many branches,
Which twist and bend and lean.

At the end of autumn,
My apples fall to the ground
And my apple tree will be bare,
Like all the trees around.

The apples that have fallen,
Will sadly be forgotten,
Lying in the overgrown grass,
Until they all turn rotten.

But there's still some life in my apple tree,
Because it's full of little nests
Which are the homes to lots of birds,
Especially, the robin redbreasts.

Tara Ogilvy (10)
Conifers School, Midhurst

Chocolate

C runchy, chewy, sticky, gooey,

H ot chocolate, cold chocolate, chop chocolate, mould chocolate,

O range chocolate is so nice, why not have a slice?

C ocoa beans are brought from foreign lands for us to have in our
own hands

O h so yummy, says my satisfied tummy

L ip-smacking, how could anyone resist it?

A ll must eat it,

T asty,

E xtra delicious.

Nairne Fraser (9)
Conifers School, Midhurst

Alone

When I went to school today
I thought it was going to be fine
But when I walked into the classroom
There were no friends of mine.

When we went out to break
I asked my friends if I could play
They said, 'Why would we want to play with you?'
I didn't know what to say.

I felt all alone
My friends didn't care
I felt all alone
No friends were there.

At the end of the day
I was so upset
I lay on my bed
And started to fret.

I cried and cried and felt so sad
How could they be so mean and bad?
I told my mum, she understood
And now I feel really good!

Joanna Charlotte Carey (9)
Conifers School, Midhurst

Frosty Mornings

Silver sparkles on crunchy,
     dewy grass.
White breath whispers in the
     cold, sharp air.
Cobwebs glisten like diamonds
     in shafts of sunshine . . .

Katie Oldworth (10)
Conifers School, Midhurst

Fish

Fish that swim in the sea,
Make funny faces at me,
They move in shoals,
Or live in holes,
It's where they like to be.

Lots of fish are blue,
Some are like you,
Other fish are shiny
And very, very tiny,
And they swim too!

Puffa fish,
Rainbow fish,
Oh and don't forget,
A nice trout dish,
It all sounds delish!

Lily Venables Kyrke (10)
Conifers School, Midhurst

Autumn Coming

Hedgehogs hibernating
Squirrels scuttling
Fires crackling
Harvest coming
Leaves crunching
Pie making
Frost biting
Colours changing
Blackberry collecting
Summer's ending!

Francesca Suter (9)
Conifers School, Midhurst

My Magic Box

(Based on 'Magic Box' by Kit Wright)

My box
Has the memories of my great grandmother
And my black cat, Dusky.
It has pictures of all my friends, family and pets.

My box
Smells of sweet lilies and petunias
It has blood-red roses for decoration
And daffodils are swaying gently.

My box
Has snow swiftly falling along with icy snowflakes
Icicles are hanging and the grass is carpeted in frost.

My box
Is lined with soft, cushiony, lilac velvet
And outside is studded with jewels.

I will treasure my box forever!

Gemma Clarke (10)
Conifers School, Midhurst

Happiness

Happiness is the smell
Of a freshly picked rose.

Happiness is hot dogs
With the ketchup oozing out.

Happiness is yellow
Like the sun.

Purdie Oldworth (9)
Conifers School, Midhurst

The Invisible Criminal

The invisible criminal,
Sneaks out at night,
Taking things that are out of our sight,
He is very hard to see
And guess what? He has come to me!

The invisible criminal,
Came last night,
He opened the door without a fight
And he didn't even use a light!

I was reading my book,
When I had a scare,
That he was actually down there!

I grabbed my pillow and crept downstairs,
Tiptoed quietly with lots of care,
But it was only the cat,
How about that!

Anja-Grace Schulp (10)
Conifers School, Midhurst

Happiness

Happiness is the delicious smell
Of warm, fresh bread.

Happiness is a midnight sky
With stars.

Happiness is silky and smooth
Like a baby's bottom.

Katherine Oliver (8)
Conifers School, Midhurst

Messy Kitchen

Flour power,
Sticky, gooey,
Eggs, water,
Doughy mixture.

Mucky fingers,
Wash them well,
Mix it up,
Make it swell.

Baking tins,
Which one to use?
Grease a tin
And heat it up.

Mixture in a tin,
Sprinkle flour on top,
Pop it in the oven -
Smells delicious!

Wait a while,
Get it out.
Voila!
We've made a cake!

Ellie Lusona-Sears (11)
Conifers School, Midhurst

Happiness

Happiness is watching butterflies play
On a beautiful, spring morning.

Happiness is the lights of a faraway city
Reflected in the sea.

Happiness is seeing my daddy's face again.

Dana Kamour (8)
Conifers School, Midhurst

Horses

I sat on the hill,
On the damp, dewy grass
And I watched the horses,
Gallop through the mist
And rest under the old oak tree,
Drinking from the stream,
As they did every morning.

What a wonderful sight they were,
White as snow,
Black as ravens,
Some chocolate brown or butter gold,
Manes flying, tails streaming,
Hooves pounding!
I felt peaceful and warm.

What a beautiful sight it was,
To see them rest under the golden oak,
Some sunbathing,
Some drinking from the cool stream,
Or grazing on the fresh, green grass.

But alas, I came and sat on the hill
And waited for the horses,
They never came. Not the next day, nor the next,
I began to lose the warm feeling inside,
My heart stopped waiting for them,
I stopped believing,
As years passed, it became a fantasy,
Just a good dream.

Maddy Sanders (10)
Conifers School, Midhurst

Autumn

A utumn leaves are falling
U nderneath the leaves are acorns
T wirling, swirling, twisting and turning
U p in the trees the colourful leaves fall
M orning dew on the grass
N ights are growing longer.

Tabitha Taylor (9)
Conifers School, Midhurst

My Magic Box
(Based on 'Magic Box' by Kit Wright)

I will put in my box . . .

An up-flowing waterfall
The distant cry of a lion
The smooth scales of a wild python
Silhouettes of galloping horses over soft sand dunes.

I will put in my box . . .

A baby's first wailing cry
The head of Frankenstein, screaming
The gunning engine of a Ferrari
An intense beam of light from a single, silver button
In the sombre night sky.

My box will be made of . . .

Fine oak-lined with mink fur
The hinges will be made of vampire's hands
Bony and thin with the grasp of a leech.

I will put my box on . . .

A deserted beach with high rolling waves
Waiting to be swallowed up.

Lauren Hayes (11)
Fletching CE Primary School, Fletching

The Three Times Table Poem

Thrice one is three
A bee holding a key.

Thrice two is six
A cat playing with bricks.

Thrice three is nine
That cow is mine.

Thrice four is twelve
My hamster saw some elves.

Thrice five is fifteen
Scruffy rats being mean.

Thrice six is eighteen
A dog smells of baked beans.

Thrice seven is twenty-one
My chicken holding a gun.

Thrice eight is twenty-four
Frogs at the door.

Grace Minney (8)
Fletching CE Primary School, Fletching

I Saw A . . .

I saw a calm ballerina rolling in muck,
I saw a hungry penguin dancing gracefully,
I saw a cheeky monkey waddle silently,
I saw a noisy stream swing from vine to vine,
I saw a delicious cookie flow down river,
I saw a glistening star grumble when I took one bite,
I saw a plump pig shining in the night sky.

Hayleigh Horscroft (11)
Fletching CE Primary School, Fletching

My Box

(Based on 'Magic Box' by Kit Wright)

I will put in my box . . .

The feel of my dog's soft, silky fur
The velvety petal of a newborn flower
The happiness and busyness of Christmas.

I will put in my box . . .

The sound of dogs barking early in the morning
The sound of trickling water in spring
The buzzing of a bee in spring
The hooting of an owl on a summer's evening
The calm lap of the sea in summer
The rustling of the trees in autumn
The first autumn conker falling to the ground
The silent plop of falling snow in winter
The winter rain on the windowpane
When I am inside, nice and warm.

I will put in my box . . .

The smell of the kitchen when my mum has been cooking
The smell of a just washed bedspread.

I will put in my box . . .

The wish that one day I will meet J K Rowling, Lucy Daniels
⠀⠀⠀⠀⠀⠀⠀⠀⠀⠀⠀⠀⠀⠀⠀⠀⠀⠀or Emma Watson
The wish that I could live forever with my family, friends and pets
The wish that I could go to New Zealand again
To see its lovely countryside, mountains and volcanoes
To touch its freezing glaciers and boiling waters
And lie on its sunny beaches again, again
The hope that I will have dogs and guinea pigs all through my life.

My box will be made of . . .

The clean, smooth silk of a newly made dress
All the colours of the rainbow
The icy, misty clouds that are in the warm, blue sky.

Georgina Lafbery (10)
Fletching CE Primary School, Fletching

My Magic Box

(Based on 'Magic Box' by Kit Wright)

I will put in my box . . .

A young Jack Russell chasing its tail
The rustling of the trees
My dad snoring in bed
A singer playing a colourful electric guitar.

I will put in my box . . .

The smell of my mum cooking cakes
The taste of ice cream
The smell of the chip shop
The taste of pasta for dinner
The smell of freshly baked pizza.

My box will be made of . . .

Gold, silver and bronze
It will have red ruby hearts on the lid
I will keep it under my bed
And when I open it,
It will feel like my horse's skin
When I ride him in the forest.

That is my magic box.

I will put in my box . . .

The shining sun blinking happily
The icy snowflakes falling on the ground
The autumn leaves falling slowly
The green grass growing in the meadow.

I will put in my box . . .

Ten more minutes in bed
Five more minutes watching telly
Two more minutes before tea is ready
And fifteen more minutes playing outside.

I will put in my box . . .

Riding on a unicorn up in the sky
Dancing with the fairy queen in my dreams
Blue sky with clouds made of candyfloss
A smiling sun setting over the sea.

I will put in my box . . .

No more wars
No more children dying with no food
No more sadness of abandoned kittens
The happiness of God shining upon us all.

That is my magic box.

Philippa Grace Penfold (10)
Fletching CE Primary School, Fletching

My Magic Box
(Based on 'Magic Box' by Kit Wright)

I will put in my box . . .

A purring kitten with soft, tabby fur
Violin's soft music playing a beautiful tune
Smell of a tulip coming out from its red bud.

My box will be made of . . .

Icicles so cold, it would burn your fingers with coldness
Colours that make your eyes shine
Secrets in the corners that can be so powerful
It can take you to the hot Amazon!

I will put in my box . . .

Delightful food of all types, like chips and strawberries
Happiness and excitement across the Atlantic ocean
The blinding light of the sun on a midsummer's afternoon.

Anneli Robinson (10)
Fletching CE Primary School, Fletching

The Magic Box
(Based on 'Magic Box' by Kit Wright)

I will put inside the box . . .

The swish of a magnificent horse's tail
The first and most brownest conker in autumn
A flower bigger than a house.

I will put inside the box . . .

A clop of a unicorn's hoof
A single spot from a Dalmatian
The tip of a pony's tail.

I will put in the box . . .

The sweet sound of a whale's call
The smell of an incense stick
The cold feel of ice cream.

My box is . . .

Light purple, the colour of happiness
The key is pure gold
The lock made from a pony's hoof.

Isabella Holopov (9)
Fletching CE Primary School, Fletching

I Saw A . . .

I saw a nutty David eating a mouse, happily,
I saw a triangular computer running fast,
I saw a massive monkey jumping forwards,
I saw an orange pig hanging upside down,
I saw a silly Ben running backwards,
I saw a blue cat eating strangely.

Alex Cove (9)
Fletching CE Primary School, Fletching

The Magic Box

(Based on 'Magic Box' by Kit Wright)

I will put in my box . . .

Hot snow going up on a summer morning
The Imperial March tune raging in the background
A deaf dog with a loving family.

I will put in my box . . .

Hundreds of Mr Kipling's strawberry slice trees
Living conkers pounding certain girls
Luke Skywalker duelling Darth Vader on the Death Star II.

My box will me made of . . .

Terror and pleasure
Happiness and sadness
Good and evil
The remnants of a star gone supernova
Bound together by mystical energy.

In my box . . .

I will duel Darth Vader to the death
Then I will defend it against the evil forces of school.

Ben Arnold (9)
Fletching CE Primary School, Fletching

I Saw A . . .

I saw a livid fire riding the skies lightly,
I saw a delicate sparrow swallow up a ship harshly,
I saw the deadly waves dance in front of the moon silkily,
I saw a beautiful wave of mist writing rhythmically,
I saw a dainty quill playing shrilly,
I saw a sparkling flute dancing elegantly!

Chantelle Evangline Cove (11)
Fletching CE Primary School, Fletching

Four Times Table

Once four is four
Found a puma on the floor.

Twice four is eight
The tiger found a mate.

Thrice four is twelve
A leopard turned into an elf.

Four fours are sixteen
I told the lion to get clean.

Five fours are twenty
The panther had plenty.

Six fours are twenty-four
Found a cheetah at the door.

Seven fours are twenty-eight
Saw a lynx outside the gate.

Eight fours are thirty-two
Saw a liger on the loo.

Nine fours are thirty-six
Spied a sphinx picking up sticks.

Ten fours are forty
Found a house cat being naughty.

Magenta Kemp (9)
Fletching CE Primary School, Fletching

I Saw A . . .

I saw a round pig slurping happily,
I saw a purple water bottle splashing crazily,
I saw a killer whale whispering softly,
I saw a dark grey teddy bear waving in the breeze loudly,
I saw a green poppy bouncing on the floor proudly,
I saw a lumpy loaf of bread plucking his hairs sadly.

Ben Sumpter (8)
Fletching CE Primary School, Fletching

My Box

(Based on 'Magic Box' by Kit Wright)

In my box I'll put . . .

The sound of a howling fox at midnight
A nightingale's song on a summer's evening
The patter of a cat's paw on a stone floor
And the sound of a waterfall in the distance.

In my box I'll put . . .

The touch of a week-old kitten's fur
The feeling of getting into a warm bath
The touch of silver spider's silk
And the feeling of a baby's soft skin.

In my box I'll put . . .

Hot rain in Antarctica
A mermaid's song
A speaking tree
And a smiling sun.

My box is made of . . .

The silk from a sparkling spider
Crystals from Mount Everest
And feathers from a golden eagle.

In my box I'll . . .

Ride on a silver bird and land on a tropical island
Where I will swim with dolphins all day
And then spend the night on the sand.

Laura Oxley (9)
Fletching CE Primary School, Fletching

My Magic Box

(Based on 'Magic Box' by Kit Wright)

I will put in my box . . .

The sound of a working cocker spaniel puppy
Barking like a monkey

I will put in my box . . .

My pony as brown as an autumn leaf

I will put in my box . . .

Lots and lots of jelly sweets.

My box will be made of . . .

Shark's teeth, as white as snow.

My box will be made of . . .

Ice shining in the sun
Clingfilm as stretchy as elastic.

I will put my box . . .

On a desk.

I will put my box . . .

In a drawer.

I will put my box . . .

Somewhere somebody will ignore.

Sarah White (9)
Fletching CE Primary School, Fletching

My Magic Box
(Based on 'Magic Box' by Kit Wright)

I will put in my box . . .

A blazing sun from the deep, blue sky
A lemur with a tail as long as a giraffe's neck
And the first purple flower shoots from the soil.

I will put in my box . . .

A sparkle of joy
The sound of a first-born baby
And a unicorn with a horn as shiny as can be.

My box will be made of . . .

A golden star as hot as the sun
The hinges are like the sharpest, shiniest tooth from a dragon's mouth
The colour blue as ripe as can be
With a sparkle of a diamond and secrets in the corners.

I will go with my box . . .

To Rome and look at all the famous places.

I will go with my box . . .

To Lapland and see Father Christmas.

I will go with my box . . .

To the hottest place on Earth and go swimming every day.

My box will stay with me forever.

Chloe Rowlinson (8)
Fletching CE Primary School, Fletching

The Three Times Table

Thrice one is three
Pineapples at the sea.

Thrice two is six
I like pears and Weetabix.

Thrice three is nine,
Kiwi fruit is fine.

Thrice four is twelve
Grapes on the shelves.

Thrice five is fifteen
The satsumas have been seen.

Thrice six is eighteen
The plums and peaches are so mean.

Thrice seven is twenty-one
Squashed bananas in a bun.

Thrice eight is twenty-four
I eat the apple core.

Thrice nine is twenty-seven
Oranges grow at Heaven.

Thrice ten is thirty
The limes are always dirty.

Cassie Galpin (10)
Fletching CE Primary School, Fletching

A Magic Box

(Based on 'Magic Box' by Kit Wright)

I will put in my box . . .

Me and my friend Regan
Watching a beautiful sunset
Listening to seagulls cry
And horses in the field below
Lovely horses
Sitting in wonderland
And the smell of the salty sea
With a green and yellow sky
And my box is in my attic
Oh I love my *magic box.*

Laura Cowling (8)
Fletching CE Primary School, Fletching

Indoors On A Rainy Day

Indoors on a rainy day,
You must act in a grown-up way.

No messing up the tidy house,
You must be quiet like a mouse.

You can't even play hide-and-seek,
Cos your little sister tends to peek.

No sliding down the bumpy stairs,
Cos Mummy says the carpet wears.

No running about all over the place,
Cos you might fall over on your face.

So indoors on a rainy day,
You must act in a grown-up way.

Amy Furlong (10)
Great Ballard School, Eartham

In My Home

Mum
My mum is very fun
Most of the time she's in the sun
Sometimes she goes to big summer parties
Her favourite foods are bags of Smarties.

Harriet
Well, what can I say about Harriet?
She's always wanted a chariot
She is so lazy
That drives me crazy
And that's the end of that.

James
James, my little brother can eat a lot
He can't even walk through a room
Without breaking a pot
He always has bad dreams
I don't normally listen
So he says I'm mean.

Me
My name is Jess
I'm always in a stress
I hate playing chess
My room's a mess
That's why my name is Jess.

Jessica Simmonds (10)
Great Ballard School, Eartham

Movement

Creeping through the spooky woods
Whatever shall I see?
Monsters, devils and bats
I wonder if they would
Turn me into a cat?

Sitting in the boring car
Waiting for what I might see
Why does it seem so far?
One hour later we are at the sea.

I am waiting in the queue
One hour and thirty minutes go by
Nearly there, but I am sitting on the pew
Trying not to cry.

Lying in my bed
Trying to get to sleep
Counting one hundred
Two hundred, three hundred sheep.

When I was a toddler
I crawled around everywhere
Under and over
Through and round stuff.

Sailing along the open water
Oh no!
We are about to crash.

Amelia Pickles (10)
Great Ballard School, Eartham

Sorry I Was Late, Miss

'Sorry I was late, Miss, but . . .
I had to watch Hayley's football match.'
'Why?' said the teacher.
'This is going to be a long story, Miss.'

'Firstly, I went to find Amelia
And then I had to wake up Anne
And Amy's gone missing, so I wanted to go and find her,
She might be alone.'

'Sorry Miss, but I have had a very stressful day so far.
I had to stop Billy from being in detention,
Hannah was dancing on the table,
Sam was late for history,
Ysabelle was too busy riding her pony,
Pelham was just being Pelham,
Matt was whinging
And Jess was being stressy.'

'So, Miss, don't tell me off.'

Clara Butterworth (10)
Great Ballard School, Eartham

Pony Club

Loading my horse up ready to go,
Jumping the jumps, *wo ho,*
I'm going round the ring in a trot,
I hope I'm going to win a lot.
I have had the greatest time of all,
I'm very lucky I did not fall.
Waiting for a dressage test,
Now I look the very best.
Now my horse is so tired,
Now he is really admired.

Ysabelle Shopland (10)
Great Ballard School, Eartham

A Dream

Me, the princess on the throne,
With gold and silver around me,
A happy, beautiful place.

From the crisp white clouds,
You can see my fairy castle,
The gardens and the fountains.

I ride the saintly unicorns,
With the knights and baronesses,
Their horns glowing brightly.

Back to the world of reality,
No fairy castle for me,
Only a deserted house with nothing but me.

The light of my room wades into my eyes,
Nothing but wet, cold, hungry me,
Only a dream.

Anne Cole (10)
Great Ballard School, Eartham

A Dragon

In the cellar is a dragon,
Who is a hundred feet tall,
With a wingspan two miles long,
Its dreadful breath,
Of fiery death,
Its claws could rip you to shreds
And teeth that could bite off your head,
But the only thing it's scared of, is a . . .
Drop of water!

Oliver Coombe-Tennant (10)
Great Ballard School, Eartham

Summer

For many different reasons,
Summer's my best of the seasons,
We lie in the sun
And have so much fun.

We paddle in the sea
And then have our tea,
We have a water fight,
It's a very funny sight.

Hayley Mackay (10)
Great Ballard School, Eartham

Football

F antastic
O ffside
O dds
T errific
B arge
A ttack
L unge
L ong ball.

Billy Darby (11)
Great Ballard School, Eartham

The Fright In The Night

One night when I was in my bed
I heard a noise inside my head
I went outside and guess what I saw?
A big house demolished right outside
I ran back upstairs to bed
In the morning, I went outside
The house was gone
It must have been a dream.

Emma Ponsford (8)
Great Ballard School, Eartham

Strike

I was reading the newspaper one day,
Looked at the headlines, hooray!
The teachers are going on strike,
I'm going to get my bike,
Now I can ride and tell my friends,
But I will have to go round bends,
First I stopped at Jessy's house,
It's a bit of a messy house,
When I told her, she shouted, 'Great!
I'm going fishing, where's the bait?'
Next I went to see Yzzy,
She is normally very busy,
When I told her she went, 'Good!
I'm going to the woods.'
Now I think I'll go and play,
I hope I will find my way.

Elisa Castro (10)
Great Ballard School, Eartham

Night-Time Friends

I heard a rustle in the wood,
I pulled on my big, furry hood,
I saw a badger behind a tree,
Snuffling at my sister's knee.
I thought I heard a very big rat!
Actually, it was my brother's pet cat!
I heard a toot,
My sister screamed!
It was an owl in a very tall tree!
I saw something leap, it made me stare,
The creature had a lot of hair.

Isla Paterson (8)
Great Ballard School, Eartham

A Fright In The Night

One night when the stars were bright,
I had a fright in the night.
I was so full of dread,
I fell out of bed.
I ran down the stairs,
With such a shock!
I wouldn't be able,
To put on my sock.
I put my wellies on
And went outside,
Guess what I found?
A grinning cat with wings like a bat,
It sat there on the mat,
'I'm not any old cat!'

Madeleine Leaver (8)
Great Ballard School, Eartham

Outside I Saw . . .

Outside I saw some mice
I saw a goblin with a dice
I shut my eyes and counted to five
I heard a noise but it was boys
I saw a broom near the moon
I saw a witch with a stick
It was a wand.
I saw a frog on a log
I saw a cat, it was black
I saw a dog, it changed into a frog
I saw a fish, in a dish
She was cooking apple pie
I said goodnight and went inside.

Harriet Simmonds (8)
Great Ballard School, Eartham

Spooky Night

The house was very frightening
Outside thunder and lightning
Everywhere was pitch black
I wish I had my friend, Jack
I crept around the house
As quiet as a mouse
I could feel things that were hairy
I hated this place, it's scary
I was feeling very weepy
Everything was so creepy
My head was full of dread
Then I found myself in bed.

Matilda Pickles
Great Ballard School, Eartham

Spooky Creatures

I thought I saw a black cat
With my witch's hat.
I looked again to see instead
A zombie rising from the dead.

It came for me as I froze in fear
I stumbled and screamed as it got near.
A bat flew out and gave me a fright
Above me it circled at quite a height.

Below a sly, sharp-eyed fox
Hurried beneath a dirty box.
That black cat I thought I saw
Wearing my witch's hat no more.

Jake Reed (8)
Great Ballard School, Eartham

The Elf

There was a young elf,
Who lived on a shelf,
He loved to eat broth
And beer with some froth.
But his favourite pastime
Was writing a rhyme.
He would write all day,
Without a word, he couldn't say.
He loved his English,
But sometimes he would wish,
He could move off that shelf,
Poor little elf!

Hannah Mason (10)
Great Ballard School, Eartham

I Feel . . .

Day 1
I feel loved but lonely,
Excited but bored,
Cosy but angry,
That's how I feel today.

Day 2
I feel joyful but jealous,
Happy but sad,
Determined but disappointed,
That's how I feel today.

Day 3
I feel funky but furious,
Super but spooked,
Down and depressed,
That's how I feel this week.

How do you feel?

Bradley Coole (10)
Heathfield Junior School, Sholing

How Do I Feel?

Sitting in my room,
Feeling gloom.
Looking into the skies,
With my two eyes.
Then looking back down,
With that horrible frown.

But soon the sun will rise
And shine into my eyes.
Forget about today,
Throw those bad thoughts away.
Cos life will be just fine,
Glorious and divine.

Day 2
Feeling great today,
Glad I threw the past away.
Feeling extravagant, no surprise,
Hanging around with all the top guys.
Amazing what one day can do,
I wonder if it's happened to you.

I feel hopeful.

Joel Whitfield (10)
Heathfield Junior School, Sholing

My Feelings

When I'm feeling sad
I think of being glad
When it comes to crying
I just can't stop sighing
All my happiness has gone away
It probably won't come back to stay.

Marie Emily Dunleavy (10)
Heathfield Junior School, Sholing

How We Feel

I feel sad when I'm alone
I feel laughter when I'm with my friends
But when they go, I'm alone again
But tomorrow they'd be back again
Can't they stay a little longer
So I can stay happy forever and ever.

Pamala Williams (10)
Heathfield Junior School, Sholing

Excited

You can smell the joyness when goals go in,
Score a joyful goal,
Do an exciting save to win the match,
But what's the point, it's only a game.

You lose a game, it's like the beginning of a game
That's against hell and not a nice day.

I feel excited when the warmth of the sun
Is surrounding me on the pitch.

Daniel Brooks (10)
Heathfield Junior School, Sholing

My Poem

Under the churchyard, six feet deep,
There lies a little mouse fast asleep.
Crept out at day and at night,
He waits to sleep before he dies.
It is war that is tragic,
Whilst a dark and bloody night.
While people sleep and mice are out of sight.
Although people die, that you love,
They will remain in your heart.

Rhys Sullivan (11)
Heathfield Junior School, Sholing

The Iceberg Of Emotions

The iceberg was as cold as a giant freezer feeling jolly.
The iceberg was as cold as the Pacific Ocean swimming
                                    for disappointment.
The iceberg was as cold as a bowling ball rolling for excitement.
The iceberg was as cold as a laughing clown.
The iceberg was as cold as a window shutting and opening
                                    for mischief.
The iceberg was as cold as a boy hoping for love.
The iceberg was determined.
The iceberg was as cold as a clock ticking away for anger.
The iceberg was as cold as a pregnant lady hurting herself.
The iceberg was as cold as a strawberry that was furious.
The iceberg was as cold as a penguin walking for the scary room.
The iceberg was as cold as a pelican that is disgusted.

Ryan Lakey (10)
Heathfield Junior School, Sholing

Monday Blues

I woke up at dawn.
Started to yawn.
Opened my eyes.
Saw a surprise.
It was a cat.
Lying on the mat.
Purring, purring.

I went in my cupboard.
Saw Miss Hubbard.
She gave me a present.
It was a pheasant.

Amanda Phillips (11)
Heathfield Junior School, Sholing

Frightened

I'm falling from a tower,
But I never hit the ground.
I try to shout and scream,
But my mouth won't make a sound.
Suddenly I see a light
That's shining towards the ground.
It must be the moon
With its beaming light,
Helping me towards the ground.

Alexandra Katie Hill (10)
Heathfield Junior School, Sholing

Loved

I feel loved when my mum gives me a kiss and a hug goodnight.
And says good morning when I wake up.
And when I hurt my leg, my mum makes it better.
Does your mum do that?

Lennie J Read (10)
Heathfield Junior School, Sholing

How I Feel

When I'm alone, I get depressed
I close my eyes and have a rest
When I'm in love, I'm on cloud nine
I feel that all the world is mine
When I am sad, I start to cry
And sit and watch the birds fly by
When I'm happy, I like to sing
And could not care about a thing
Emotions come and go each day
And we all feel them in every way.

Matthew Burt (10)
Heathfield Junior School, Sholing

I Love . . .

I love my family, so soft and sweet,
They help me through problems as if I cheat.

I love their faces, they make me shiver,
I love their souls, they make me quiver.

My family is just great,
That's who *I love!*

Bethany Thomson (10)
Heathfield Junior School, Sholing

How I Feel

Looking around,
The world's turned upside down.
Feeling sad and very mad,
My day outside was very bad.
By soon the sun will shine,
Everything will be just fine.
Feeling great,
Just can't wait.
Playing on my PS2,
Has this ever happened to you?

Brandon Dawson (10)
Heathfield Junior School, Sholing

I Feel . . .

When I am sad, I feel so mad
When I am happy, I feel so glad
When I feel sick, I wish I was a stick
And when I am at school, I am a witch
I don't get why and I don't get how
But that's life and that is fine.

Ashleigh Houghton (10)
Heathfield Junior School, Sholing

How I Feel

I feel sad
When I'm mad,
I feel a fool
When I'm cool,
I feel rich
When I'm a witch,
I feel like a mouse
When I'm a house,
But when I feel happy
I feel like me!
I feel like a shirt
When I'm eating dirt,
I feel like a shed
When I'm dead,
I feel cruel
When I say a rule,
I feel like a dolly
When I eat a lolly,
But when I feel sad
I feel like a loner!

Conor Whyte (10)
Heathfield Junior School, Sholing

Spooked

Last night in the hall,
I heard sounds around the school,
I'm sure it was not the ball.

The bats came out at night,
They gave me an awful fright
And then I knew I had to fight.

But then I saw the gigantic snake,
I began to shake,
Then I saw the ground quake . . .

Thomas Williams (10)
Heathfield Junior School, Sholing

When I'm Upset

When I'm upset I forever cry
And don't know why
And feel like I can fly.

When I'm upset I forever cry
And wish I could die.

When I'm upset I forever cry
And wonder why, why, why, why?

When I'm upset I forever cry
And sit and sigh.

But when I'm upset I forever cry
Look at the sky and sigh
Float up there and fly as I cry
Upset to the sunset.

Michael Watts (10)
Heathfield Junior School, Sholing

Anger

Anger bubbles up inside you
Like something my mum would cook.
It makes you stare at things
Then stop and look.
It makes you jump like thunder.
It is bright and sparkly
And frightening like lightning.
It is hot and bursts like a volcano.
It's like my sister (the insane-o!)
It is dark and lurks in the shadows.
It pushes you every corner you turn.
It is like a hawk, always following you.
It's a big pool of fire.
I will say it again and again.
Anger is inside you and it always will be.

Lauren Hobbs (10)
Heathfield Junior School, Sholing

The Life Game

When I look at the sky
Calmness stares at me, eye to eye.
I feel like I'm floating right up there
I feel like I'm floating in the air.
Here comes anger flying by
I feel livid with that guy.
I feel so sad and that's a shame
I never get sad with a game.
Now I'm happy once again
'Cause here comes the sunshine, gone is the rain.
Once again here I am
Floating right up there
Floating in the air!
Floating . . . floating . . .

Bethany Doyle (10)
Heathfield Junior School, Sholing

Black And White

Black is the colour of the night.
Lilac is the colour of space.
Amber is the colour of the middle traffic light.
Cream is the colour of my dog.
Clear is the colour of a pane of glass.

Azure is the colour of the blue sky.
Indigo is the colour of nothing.
Dark red is the colour of the first traffic light.

White is the colour of paper.
Hazel is the colour of eyes.
Indigo is the colour of my screen saver.
Turquoise is the colour of the Mediterranean sea.

George Farrar
Hordle Walhampton School, Walhampton

Black And White

As black as night he soared
I stood no chance
But for my adored
I must joust.
There was he
The Devil's knight
But for the key
I must fight.
All night we charged
But none could win
They'll sing a bard
I'll fight against sin.
Then I smashed
With one last yell
Against his armour
And yes, he fell.
I had won
I'd got my key
'I found my son'
Lost had he.

Michael Truell (11)
Hordle Walhampton School, Walhampton

Black And White

Black, dark clouds all around
What does this mean?

White, I can't see anything
Pearly Gates
What does this mean?

Looking down I see them crying
What have I done?
Who was I?

Soraya Allen (12)
Hordle Walhampton School, Walhampton

Black And White

John Dick Smith was the man who pushed her
Darling Bess, our oldest Sister.
Born as a common girl, raised up for work,
The hardest tasks she ne'er would shirk.
Came to the nunnery, in dead of night,
Her placid white face quite shaken with fright.
'Oh Mother!' she cried at our Superior's feet,
'I've wronged so badly, to you I must weep!'
The old mother smiled, God bless her sleeping soul
And beckoned her in, away from the cold.
From there our Bess lived, the sweetest of dears,
To her we did run to show her our fears.
Then one day, a knock rapped at the old door,
Our Bess, aged eighty, crept 'cross the floor.
A shriek was heard and then there was none,
We rushed to the sound, but yet it was gone.
At the bottom of the slope, that led down to the sea,
Our Bess was now lying, still as could be.
Then man, it turned out, who came that day,
Was the very same man who had led Bess astray.
All those years past, when she had come to escape,
Her man had got her and killed her poor shape.
Whatever happened, that long time ago,
That the good Lord, we never shall know.
John Dick Smith was the man who pushed her,
Darling Bess, our oldest Sister.

Lucy Ogilvie
Hordle Walhampton School, Walhampton

Black And White

The white ball shining,
From the floodlights of the stadium,
The black sky stands out,
From the light of the pitch,
My black and white flashback,
Of my friend being out,
Now I'm in,
I will not disappoint.

The frightening black shadows,
Of the players on the field,
The umpire raises his finger
And I'm out of here!

Jamie Gossage (11)
Hordle Walhampton School, Walhampton

Black And White

A black and a white man
Reading black and white papers
On a black and white bench
In a black and white alley
Near a black and white road
Beside a black and white house
With a black and white roof
Under black and white clouds
In a black and white world
In a black and white space
Will he ever see
The colours in the world?

Charlie Skinner (12)
Hordle Walhampton School, Walhampton

Black And White

Black and white,
Stars at night.
Contrasting colours,
That move the heart.

The ebony and ivory,
Combine in perfect harmony.
The unlucky magpie,
Sits alone in the tree.

A tornado passing by,
Causes darkening of the sky.
Great big polar bears,
Stalk their prey in the icy Arctic.

Fluffy white clouds brighten the sky,
Following the tornado passing by.
Is there hope for the future?
Can there be?
We don't know!

Laura Wiltshire (11)
Hordle Walhampton School, Walhampton

Black And White

Imagine you were a chess piece
Would you choose to be black or white?
If you moved, which square would you move to?
Black or white?
Which would you choose?
Imagine you were picking a magazine
Would you choose to buy black or white?
Would you read it if it was black and white?
Which would you choose?
Have a think?

Marco Mills (12)
Hordle Walhampton School, Walhampton

Black And White

Black and white cats in the sky,
Scratching by and by,
Their flashy personalities are so sly,
When they come across a dog,
They *miaow* to the moonlight,
When they're gentle and they're nice,
You just have to give them mice.

Lubinda Lishomwa (8)
Hordle Walhampton School, Walhampton

Black And White

Black is like a stealth fighter
Moving in the sky.

White is like a rocket
Going to the moon.

Black is like a blackbird
Gliding through the sky.

White is like an aeroplane
Taking off at noon.

Ben Willis (12)
Hordle Walhampton School, Walhampton

Black And White

My dog is black
His name is Jack.
My cat is white
She likes to fight.

Jack takes flight
To avoid a fight.
And the cat
Came running after.

Emily Orford (8)
Hordle Walhampton School, Walhampton

Black And White

My cat is white and black
He likes to wrap in his mat
In his cage he likes to play
With his bell which rings all day

My dog is black and white
He likes to bark at people
And bite them.

Bree Roberts (8)
Hordle Walhampton School, Walhampton

Black And White

Photos are light
Photos are dark
Photos are good
Photos are bad

Photos of cats
Photos of dogs
Photos of whales
And skunk tails.

Tara Clapham (8)
Hordle Walhampton School, Walhampton

Black And White

My friend has got a magpie
He feeds it skates
On the other hand
He's got a black and white cat
Called Black Beard
Black Beard always tries
To jump from the black sofa
Up to the white shelf onto the black cage
And falls with a bump and into his cage to rest.

Ben Crane (9)
Hordle Walhampton School, Walhampton

War Of Night And Day

The black of night comes
out of sunlight blackening
every ray of sunlight.

The white of the street light
light going dim on the
blackened streets for the
revenging light.

The rays of light depart for
the revenge of light
depart for night so black but
no light.

The first shine makes war
again for the mistake is made
for the sun goes around the world
and will not stop the
world's fate.

Humphrey Bonsor (9)
Hordle Walhampton School, Walhampton

Black And White

Black and white bells are ringing
Black and white birds are singing
Black and white cats are sitting
Black and white rats are squeaking
Black and white cars are beeping.

Black and white girls are speaking
Black and white boys are peeking
Black and white trees are creaking
Black and white ceilings are leaking
Black and white zebras are springing.

Shane Devlin (11)
Hordle Walhampton School, Walhampton

Black And White

I have a Dalmatian who's potty
Because he is very spotty
He ran away, but that's okay
Cos I've got a new dog called Dotty.

Then Dotty ran off
With a black and white winged moth
And a fat, old, ugly zebra
And a shy, young badger called Debra.

Hannah Lees (8)
Hordle Walhampton School, Walhampton

A Skunk!

I'm black and white with a bushy tail
If I'm cornered, without fail
I'll spray you!

Keep your distance, for when I spray
Clothes will have to be thrown away!

Skunk is my name, a creature small
I wonder why people don't like me at all?

Guy Wilkinson (8)
Hordle Walhampton School, Walhampton

Black And White

Skunks make a smell if they want to defend themselves
Zebras can run fast, they have stripes.
Rabbits eat grass
Their back legs are like springs.

Cats can be very good, sometimes they will let you pick them up
Panda bears eat bamboo, they live in a nest of bamboo.
Horses can run fast and jump, horses live in a stable
Dogs are furry, their paws are soft.

Georgina Lewis (8)
Hordle Walhampton School, Walhampton

Black And White

Black dog, white mouse
Woof, woof, squeak, squeak,
Animals all around.

Black cat, white bunny
Who can you spot in the night?
'Not me,' says the cat, 'only in the light.'

My name is Punk
Guess what? I am a black and white skunk
But please don't tell
I like to make a very big smell.

My horse is black and white
So you can see him in the night
Especially when the moon is bright
Which is a delight!

Marina McWhirter (8)
Hordle Walhampton School, Walhampton

Black And White

Black and white skunks,
Smell like a load of punks.
Every single penguin,
Can swim and waddle
And sometimes they have a paddle.

Killer whales are black and white,
They are not very bright.
Magpies have only two wings
And they like collecting things.

Joshua Rehel (8)
Hordle Walhampton School, Walhampton

Black And White

The shadows of night
come out.
You could be dead
or maybe instead
you're tucked up in bed.

The shadows of night
have a fight
over some moulded brain.

The shadows of night
win the fight as the evil of
black and white
come out at night.

James Dare (10)
Hordle Walhampton School, Walhampton

Black And White

My cat is black
Black as midnight
No, no, not white as moonlight.

Black clouds in the sky
Always scurry by
Clouds are white
White as snow.

Clouds are fluffy
So fluffy you could
Sleep on one.

Rachel Lee (8)
Hordle Walhampton School, Walhampton

Black And White

From flying magpies
To stinky skunks
They all have one thing in common
They're all black and white.

I'm feared all over the world
I'm also very stinky
I'm a skunk
That's me.

I've very good at swimming
I waddle quite a lot
I'm a penguin
That's me.

Harry Vokins (8)
Hordle Walhampton School, Walhampton

Black And White

A porcupine is black and white
Be careful not to get a spike
In your finger.
If you do, it hooks
And then it won't come out,
No matter if you cry and shout.
His spikes are black and white,
Normally he lives in a cave
In the country.

Orlando Kary (8)
Hordle Walhampton School, Walhampton

Black And White

Zebras, pandas, penguins and badgers
All of a colour of black and white,
They creep and they crawl
And they're furry and small.

Zebras striped black and white,
Penguins in sections,
Pandas have patches,
Badgers are scavengers,
Skunks are smelly,
Porcupines are spiky,
Because his name's Mikey!

Arabella Gamble (11)
Hordle Walhampton School, Walhampton

Black And White

There was a ghost
who'd always boast
that it came in the post.

There was a bear
that ate a pear
with a hare.

There was a snake
that was caught in a rake
while eating steak.

There was a dodo that
used to go-go, until it got a pogo.

Charlie Banks (10)
Hordle Walhampton School, Walhampton

Black And White

Cloudy is a pony,
She is grey as grey
As grey, she never
Stays clean, you
See she is always
In the mud.

She jumps so high
So safely
She will never
Make you scared
She can be bad
When she doesn't
Get her own way.

She gets going when
I'm around because
I give her a smack
When I get on her
She is always
On her toes
Sometimes she goes
Too fast
I can barely stop.

But I sit back
And enjoy the ride
Sometimes I do
Jumps.

Isabella Wallrock (8)
Hordle Walhampton School, Walhampton

Once Upon A Rhyme

Once upon a rhyme
it's quite a funny story
I landed back in time
I met a man called Cory.
Called himself Cory Makespeare
It was quite a fact
You should be called William Shakespeare
You really should be sacked.
I found myself with Henry
He was the 8th, but was the 2nd
Which should be contemporary
You got to reckon
He should have chopped his head
Like he did to his wives
Which are happily dead
With his shiny, chopping knives.
I reckon he should have been a mate
Who died of cancer
Two years late.

Harry Tatner (10)
Oakfield Primary School, Totton

Love

Love makes me very happy inside.
It's the colour of dark pink roses.
It smells like Valentine's Day.
Love reminds me of my family because I love them.

I think love is like a rich ruby.
It's like the sunset.
Love feels like a juicy strawberry.
It tastes like a box of chocolates.
Love sounds like peaceful music.
It reminds me of the sun shining all day.

Hattie Rawlins (8)
Oakwood School, Oakwood

Darkness

Darkness, I love darkness
Because it makes me feel spooky
And excited all over
I think it is fun.

I can see shadows lurking in the trees
It is as cold as ice
I think it is mischievous
And cold black is its colour.

It is cold and calm in the gloom
It is curling the trees in the salty air
I think it is dusty
I think it smells like fire burning
I think it tastes like liquorice laces
It makes me feel happy.

Toby Allison (8)
Oakwood School, Oakwood

Darkness

I like darkness because it's spooky and dark
There's shadows all around me.

Darkness is cold and spooky
Creepy like a hole in your tummy.

It tastes like rotten cheese
With stinky sauce with stinky fish.

It smells like old air
With rotten pizza and ketchup on top.

When I look around me
I see darkness everywhere.

I love darkness
It's dark and black, misty sky.

Alexander Russell (8)
Oakwood School, Oakwood

My Family

I love my family, they are kind and helpful.
I love them all and I love my cats.
They are tabby ones.
One is called Mitsey and the other's Calico, she is fat.

I love my mum, she is kind and loves me.
She is a teacher and teaches food technology.
She cooks lovely food.
She is the best!

My brother is kind
And goes to Churchers College.
He is very clever
And in the top set of nearly everything.

My cats are cute and soft.
They purr very loudly.
I love them all.
Purr, purr!

I love my family.
I love my family.
I love my family!

Katie Sharp (9)
Oakwood School, Oakwood

Darkness

Darkness is spooky like a foggy graveyard.
Darkness is a creepy castle that is deserted.
Darkness is as cold as a pond with ice on it.
Darkness is as black as midnight.

Darkness is as evil as a robber.
Darkness is as salty as a seaside.
Darkness is as quiet as a mouse.

Darkness is like a spider inside my tummy.
Darkness is like aliens invading my home.

Faith Withinshaw (8)
Oakwood School, Oakwood

Anger

I hate anger.
It makes me go red in the face.
It feels like I have eaten a red chilli
Because my mouth is hurting
And I don't know what to do with my brother
Who I am shouting at.

It sounds like drums banging and banging
It goes on and on.
Anger is the colour of a red strawberry.
It smells of coal burning on a hot, red fire.
It reminds me of volcanoes erupting
Throwing out puffs of smoke.
I hate anger.
It is horrid because I prefer happy people.

Natasha Morgan (9)
Oakwood School, Oakwood

Darkness

Darkness is as black as midnight
It reminds me of a spooky graveyard
Filled with vampires and creepy crawlies
The fresh air is cold, foggy and all you can hear are owls hooting.

Ordinary noises sound spooky in darkness
People have nightmares
Darkness tastes like chocolate
It smells like salty air.

Darkness feels like a soft cushion
It is the colour of a black diamond
Darkness destroys all the light
But the end of darkness is a new day.

Georgiana Osborn (8)
Oakwood School, Oakwood

Happiness

Happiness looks like a garden of flowers
All pretty and pink.
Happiness feels like a fluffy, little chick
Just cracked in my hands.

Happiness sounds like a child laughing.
Happiness reminds me of when my family are smiling.
Happiness tastes like sticky, sweet honey.

Happiness smells like a big chocolate cake.
Happiness is gold, like the happy sunshine.
Happiness is a shooting star flying across the Earth.

Happiness is a big box of chocolates.
Happiness is having a pet to love.
Happiness is warming up in front of a fire on a wet, cold day.

Emily Hutchin (8)
Oakwood School, Oakwood

Sadness

I hate sadness because it . . .

Smells like tears shed from an unhappy child.
It smells like burnt polystyrene on a wet, cold day.
Smells as sad as a child that has lost his brother.
It feels as cold as if you have been teased, bullied,
Lost a World Cup and a mother has lost her baby.
A grey cloud feels like you have lost your best friend
And been dumped by a horrible girl who has taken all your money.
I get sad when my friends take my things
And I feel sad when people are tortured
And *I hate it* when I see people pollute the world.

Dominic Wood (9)
Oakwood School, Oakwood

Happiness

Happiness is amber dancing in a field
It is soft like my friends' voices
It feels like baby bunnies
It sounds like a piano playing softly.

Happiness is warm like the sun
It tastes like honey melting in my mouth
It is a chick in a nest
It smells like butter melting on hot toast
It looks like a twinkling star
It is a happy dream.

Happiness makes me joyful
And warm inside
It makes me want to jump
I have happiness when I have chocolate.

Ellen Lavender (8)
Oakwood School, Oakwood

Darkness

I hate the darkness because it's scary.
It is fun when it's Bonfire Night.
The dark is as black as a bull
And as shiny as an ebony stone.

The darkness is like a path that never ends.
It feels like a statue of a horse that looms above me.

Dark is like a dark man trying to catch me
I run and run as fast as I can.
But what's this? The man is gone
This is the end of my darkness.

George Cunningham (8)
Oakwood School, Oakwood

My Papa

When I'm with my papa
I am safe and sound.
Sometimes we laugh
And then have a run-around.
He helps me with my math
And even cleans my shoes.
Papas are great
Don't you think so too?

Brontë Graham (9)
Oakwood School, Oakwood

Anger

Anger feels like hot, burning lava bubbling in my stomach.
Anger sounds like someone roaring in my ear.
It looks like coal taken from a fire.
It tastes like orange mints crunching in my mouth.

Anger is the colour of blood when you cut yourself.
Anger reminds me of a rock band gone bad.
It smells like burning plastic on a bonfire.
It makes me think of death.

Louisa Filary (9)
Oakwood School, Oakwood

My Hamster

Spotty skin, like a Dalmatian.
Tiny eyes and a small button nose.
Big belly, like a fluffy cushion.
Big, fat cheeks in which to store its food.
Running around on its wheel all day.
This is how he plays.

Olivia Sumner (9)
Oakwood School, Oakwood

Golf

Golf is a quiet game.
It makes you strong.
The ball is white.
Hole in one, someone said.
That's gone far.
Every second you hear
Smash! Whoosh! Click!

Jack Sheeran (9)
Oakwood School, Oakwood

The Well

A cold, wet well
It feels like rock
As strong as bricks
It is damp and deep.
It looks like it goes on forever.
The water is crystal clear.
Ice-cold drinking water.
It sounds like an empty world.

Guy Mansell (9)
Oakwood School, Oakwood

My Cat

My cat is warm and cuddly.
I can hold him in my hands.
He is very silly.
I play with him as much as I can.
He is the size of my foot.
I love my cat!

Elli Lytton (9)
Oakwood School, Oakwood

Violence

Violence is mean
You can lose your loved ones.

It's so horrid
It's like your family has gone forever.

The sun is blocked by the moon
And you can't see where you are going.

You carry weapons of destruction.
It could destroy your whole life.

It's so dangerous.
You would let your whole family down.

It smells disgusting
Like jam and marmalade mixed together.

Robbie Holden (9)
Oakwood School, Oakwood

Darkness

Darkness reminds me of a foggy graveyard
Lurking in the distance.
Darkness is as strong as lightning.

Darkness smells of burning leaves.
Darkness sounds like someone screaming.
Darkness is gloomy and scary.
It is also dusty and cold.

Darkness looks like a devil
With fire on his face.
Darkness is evil.

George Hamilton-Green (9)
Oakwood School, Oakwood

Anger

Anger is horrible and it makes me unhappy.
It's like a big drum, banging.
Anger is as strong as the wind.
Anger is as great as a king.

Anger smells like hot ash.
Anger is like a gun being shot.
Anger is in every place.
People don't know this.

Anger is as horrible as a robber.
Anger tastes like a red stone.
Anger is a hot devil.
I hate anger.

Alec Walker (8)
Oakwood School, Oakwood

Love

Love is pink like roses
Like pink and red flowers in a garden
Like a sun setting.

Love is a box of chocolates and a single red rose
Like sweet peas
Like moonlight.

Love is flowers blooming in spring
Like sweets in a sweet shop
Like sunlight.

Love is all those things
But to me, love is kind.

Laura Greenfield (8)
Oakwood School, Oakwood

Fear

Fear is grey, grey as ash.
It is an owl that hoots in the dark.
Fear tastes like a rotten apple.
Fear reminds you of a black cave.

Fear feels like a cold, slimy thing.
It puts a gasp where a smile would be.
It is the moon hidden behind a cloud.
Fear smells like ash that is still burning.

Fear tastes like dark as black as midnight.
Fear makes you run even if you don't want to.
It makes me as white as a sheet.

Harriet Field (9)
Oakwood School, Oakwood

Anger

Anger is as green as grass.
It tastes of burning fire straight from the fireplace.
My heart's beating very fast
The sound of footsteps is coming closer and closer.

It looks like lava is whizzing out.
The wind's blowing the country, round and round.
Someone's crushing the world to bits.

It reminds me of an ambulance zooming down the road.
It feels like you have got hurt very badly and you're crying with pain.
It also feels like there's an adventure coming up.

Harry Johnson (8)
Oakwood School, Oakwood

Kindness

Kindness smells like fresh honey.
Kindness tastes of someone's laughter.
Kindness looks like a bird singing.
It feels like a bouncy cloud.
It glows in the moonlight.

It is as blue as a sapphire ring.
It reminds me of when my family are together.
It sounds like the fireworks going off on Bonfire Night.

It is in everyone in the world.
I love kindness.
It makes me eat a thousand chocolates
And then brush my teeth.

Innes Hopkins (8)
Oakwood School, Oakwood

Dolphin

He can hear if there is another dolphin calling him.
He can taste it if he eats something poisonous.
When there is a boat coming, he can smell it.
He has small, little eyes like a human.
He feels silky in the water.
He is soft just like a rabbit.
He swims as fast as a cheetah.
He hides behind a rock
And when a fish goes past
He eats it!

Victoire Michel (9)
Oakwood School, Oakwood

Football

It is as light as a mushroom.
You can enjoy the fresh air.
It keeps you fit.
The ball is black and white.
It is a challenge.
It is very fun in school.
It is good to play for your team.
It is fun if you win.

Josh Brooke-Jones
Oakwood School, Oakwood

My Cat, Harry

Harry cat.
My cat, Harry, has soft black and white, silky fur.
Every night I cuddle him
And he feels like a black and white piece of fluff.
He makes the sound of a mouse sleeping.
He smells like a vase of roses.
When the dog comes, he pounces.
He is the best cat in the world.

Daisy Strange (9)
Oakwood School, Oakwood

My Kitten

My kitten is called Screeches
And he smells of peaches.
When he is in a good mood
I give him kitten food.
I give him milk
To make his fur like silk.

Travis Torode (9)
Oakwood School, Oakwood

The Lion

It runs as fast as lightning.
Its roar is louder than thunder.
Its teeth are as sharp as knives.
It can see some prey 300 yards away.
Its teeth are sharp and scary.
Its yellow mane blows in the wind.

Henry Foster (9)
Oakwood School, Oakwood

Barney, My Dog

Barney's smile is like the sun shining in the sky.
He loves the taste of meat.
Barney is as fluffy as a cloud
And his ears are as soft as velvet.
Barney's sense of smell is so good
He can smell food from miles away.
Barney's bark is as loud as a roaring lion.

Jamie Munro (9)
Oakwood School, Oakwood

The Minotaur

I'm the depressed Minotaur
I'm lonely and sad
I'm half bull and half man
And I am not all that glad
I will die of thirst and hunger
I need some flesh
My dagger-like horns scraping against people's chests.

Charlotte Higby (10)
Ocklynge County Junior School, Eastbourne

Scared

Horrified
Terrified
Freaked out
Shuddering
Shivering
Shuddering.

Kyle Whittlesey (9)
Ocklynge County Junior School, Eastbourne

Loneliness

Upset
Sad
Stuck
Isolated
Alone
Cross.
Ugh!

Kitty Nielsen (9)
Ocklynge County Junior School, Eastbourne

Scared

Teeth
Chatter
Heart
Thumping
Jelly
Legger
Hands
Quiver
Give
A shiver
Spooky!

Hollie Wilkins (9)
Ocklynge County Junior School, Eastbourne

Angry

Annoyed
Furious
Frustrated
Mad
Totally red
A kick
A punch
I jump
On my
Bed.

Tom Pashley (9)
Ocklynge County Junior School, Eastbourne

Careworn

Unhappy
Sorrowful
Crestfallen
Glum
Grave
Desolate
Down
Careworn.

Chris Maskill (9)
Ocklynge County Junior School, Eastbourne

Annoyed

Teeth clenched
Fists too
I see red
Blood runs blue
Eyes swollen
Try to move
Annoyed!

Jessica Woodrow (9)
Ocklynge County Junior School, Eastbourne

Feelings Happy

Smile
Laugh
Excited
Kind
Helpful
Gentle
Funny
Bright
And
Me!

Gary Fry (9)
Ocklynge County Junior School, Eastbourne

The Minotaur

I want to be loved in this world.
Why won't people care for me?
Okay, so I have a bull's head,
But don't take me from the outside,
Take me from the inside.

Jason Taylor (11)
Ocklynge County Junior School, Eastbourne

Happy

Happy
Cheerful
Smiling
Laugh
Giggle
Talking with
Friends
Happiness.

Leah Kiely (9)
Ocklynge County Junior School, Eastbourne

The Minotaur

I'm lonely beyond belief,
I'm starving to death.
Every seven years,
Fourteen children are sent
Who I've got to eat, or I'll die.
My hair is wet and gets everywhere.
I'm half covered in blood!
This place, I wouldn't call it home, stinks.
It's so puzzling, I keep getting lost.
My left horn hurts so badly,
I've got to hold it tightly to ease the pain.
My arms don't feel right
And gosh! Does my neck ache!
I wonder what it's like outside.
It's got to be better than this dark, damp and doomed maze.
I hate it!
I'll be in this boring and gloomy dungeon till I die!
Please, please, can someone help me?

Curtis Mays (10)
Ocklynge County Junior School, Eastbourne

Sad

Careworn
Cheerless
Crestfallen
Dejected
Upset
Discontented
Disappointed
Guilty
Grieving
Discouraged
Disheartened
Woeful.

Michelle Turner (9)
Ocklynge County Junior School, Eastbourne

The Minotaur

I'm the Minotaur.
People hate me.
Why do I have to be in this labyrinth?
It smells like a toilet.
How can I make friends?
Why am I lonely?
I'll soon be killed.
My only friend is my human sister,
She doesn't come that often.
On my list for food is rats' tails, webs and chewed bone.
I get fed every seven years.
My eyes freeze.
I wish I had fish and chips.
No one gives me water.
I'll kill King Minos,
I'll have my revenge - *roar!*
Watch out Minos, I'm after you!
Please help me,
I'll help you.

David Purton (10)
Ocklynge County Junior School, Eastbourne

The Minotaur

I am the fierce Minotaur,
My horns as sharp as daggers,
My coat as firm as rock,
My head is bull,
My body is man,
All I have is bones to chew,
The tunnel's as cold as snow,
The walls as green as grass.

Anna-Marie Wright (10)
Ocklynge County Junior School, Eastbourne

Moving House

It's such a big rush,
Just running around,
Packing everything that's found,
We're in such a rush, can't you hear the sound?
I don't want to go,
I want to stay here,
I've got one great tear
And I'm filled with fear.
I don't want to leave my friends,
I'll be round too many bends,
We'll miss chatting about the latest trends.
Making new friends is what I fear most,
Who will I think about when I butter my toast?
Who will I meet in the morning at the post?
      Goodbye dear friend,
      But this isn't the end.

Roxy Knights (11)
Ocklynge County Junior School, Eastbourne

The Minotaur

Here I am, lying in my dark, dismal labyrinth,
Waiting for another seven miserable years to go by.
I'm half-starved and my red, bloody horns
Are waiting for another brainless human to torture and execute.
My petrifying, orange eyes
Haven't seen the brightness of day for decades.
My human body struggles to lift my head,
Which is of a bull.
My lion-shaped teeth are gradually growing weaker
And my sudden headaches are getting worse.
So I'm waiting for another seven years till I'm fed.
Trust me, that's torture.

William McIntyre (10)
Ocklynge County Junior School, Eastbourne

The Minotaur

I swagger around, longing for someone
To end my seemingly everlasting misery
And my weapon is no use for protecting me
From my anguished self.

I'm misunderstood as I lurk in my labyrinth,
An enemy of the world, by no means loved.
I wait every year for my prey to come forth,
Ravenous for my supper.
The stench of my breath
Is enough to overwhelm my visitors.

I'm miserable, lonely, agonized to the bone
And I take my anger out
On the humans that come my way,
Needle-sharp horns sinking into their flesh.

I hear their screams, echoing,
Bouncing off the slimy walls.
I'm grotesquely hideous and as I see my reflection
In the pool of blood lying at my feet,
I turn away in shame at the monster I've become.

I'm tormented every day,
With the pain searing through me.
I am the Minotaur,
The beast that haunts your days and nights.

Lucy Gray (10)
Ocklynge County Junior School, Eastbourne

The Gorgon Medusa

I live at the end of the world with my three sisters.
My wild hair rustles with poisonous snakes.
I have red, glaring eyes, flashing like thunder.
They will turn you to stone.
My skin is a slimy green colour, like a toad's.

Rachael Reed (10)
Ocklynge County Junior School, Eastbourne

The Minotaur

I am the Minotaur,
Friendless and alone,
Bored and lonely and nowhere to go.
The smell of death
Lingers on my breath.
No one there to help me.
I live in a labyrinth
That's dark and cold,
I'm half man, half bull.
I'm dying more and more each day
And I'm starving most of the time.
Who will end this wretched life of mine?
I'm sad because nobody likes me,
They say I'm foul.
I feed on humans, that's probably why,
But all I want to do is die.

Jessica Clarke (10)
Ocklynge County Junior School, Eastbourne

The Minotaur

I am the Minotaur,
I have no love, I just have hate.
Every day my body lies beneath the damp, cold labyrinth,
My neck in agony from my straining head.
Day by day, week by week, year by year I beg for sunlight,
But I get a dark, gloomy maze
Which my horns bang, clang and scrape against.
Venom is poisoning my throat.
Who will end my misery?
Who will change my future?
How will I die?

Jamie Sivers (10)
Ocklynge County Junior School, Eastbourne

The Minotaur

I am the most venomous creature you have ever smelt.
I am always lonely, waiting for people to come and end my misery.

I'm half man, half bull,
Half flesh, half fur,
Living in the cold, damp and dismal labyrinth.

I always have saliva dripping out of my muzzle.
If someone comes into my labyrinth,
They will never come out!

I have two horns on top of my head,
Right above my red, glowing eyes.
I am like a monster from a faraway planet.

So, please do not, I repeat *do not*
Go into my labyrinth,
Or you will never, ever, ever come out!

Hannah Barnato-Ludbrook (10)
Ocklynge County Junior School, Eastbourne

The Minotaur

I'm the Minotaur,
Waiting day after day
In this dirty, disgusting, dark dungeon,
The damp walls crushing my foul, scraggy, hairy arms,
With no friends at all,
Searching for food that's been waiting for years,
Ripping a lamb, tearing it apart bit by bit,
As my yellow venom horns curve round,
Pushing down on my knotted, blood-dripping head.
I roar, feeling sorry for myself, hoping to be dead,
Waiting years and years and still no love.

Charlotte White (10)
Ocklynge County Junior School, Eastbourne

The Minotaur

I am the Minotaur,
With not a friend in the world.

I am the lonely Minotaur,
My heart broken long ago.

I am the angry Minotaur,
Seeking revenge.

I hate the smell of death on my breath
And the taste of blood on my tongue.

The dark, lonesome labyrinth,
It's enough to put anyone off.

Innocent bodies lying on the floor
And the scent of rotting flesh.

I am the revolting Minotaur,
With my head disproportionate to the rest of my body.

I am the ugly Minotaur,
Waiting to die.

Nathan Visick (10)
Ocklynge County Junior School, Eastbourne

The Minotaur

I'm a friendless Minotaur, not a friend in the world.
I live in a dingy, damp labyrinth.
I'm starving because I only get fed every seven years.
My bull-head horns scrape on the low ceiling,
My twisted iron club ready to hit you,
My rough and ragged hooves crank on the floor.
I'm anguished and hate myself.
I am the Minotaur.
Who will end my misery?

Matthew Stace (10)
Ocklynge County Junior School, Eastbourne

The Minotaur

Every second of my life is agony,
Friendless, lonely.
My breath smells of death.
I lie in misery, half starved in a prison of Hell,
Anguished and alone in my dark, dismal labyrinth.
My fangs can tear through steel.
I'm half man, half bull.
My neck strains to hold my head.
My warm, venomous breath wafts around me.
My horns rip through the rock of the ceiling.
Every seven years I feed on seven humans.
I'm crazed in agony,
Just waiting to die,
So who will end my anguished life?

Nicole Hoddinott (10)
Ocklynge County Junior School, Eastbourne

The Minotaur

I am the Minotaur, friendless and alone.
My loneliness makes me feel dismal.
I hate myself 'cause I live in a dungeon.
Who will end my misery?

I am the Minotaur, friendless and alone.
The labyrinth is so miserable.
I've been here for so many years now.
Who will end my misery?

I am the Minotaur, friendless and alone.
I'm bored stiff, as they say,
Wishing to be free of this dump.
Who will end my misery?

Emma Thursfield (10)
Ocklynge County Junior School, Eastbourne

The Minotaur

I am the gruesome Minotaur,
Friendless and alone.
I'm stuck down in the labyrinth,
To kill all those who enter.

I'm half bull, half man,
Half human flesh, half beast
And I'm rotting from pure loneliness
Which I hope you never know.

I am fed every seven years
On innocent Athenians.
I roar and bellow, they scream with pain
As my horns penetrate the heart.

The corridors are dark and dank,
Repulsive and quite putrid.
My thoughts have wandered them many times,
Trying to find an exit.

Once again, I am the lonely Minotaur
And death would be quite welcome.
So if you hear this prayer of death,
Come, help me out of this prison.

Lily Stoneley (10)
Ocklynge County Junior School, Eastbourne

The Minotaur

I am the Minotaur and I wish that I had a friend,
But I am the Minotaur and no one would be a friend
To a half man and half bull,
And no one would even live
In my dark, cold, damp, dismal and miserable home.
Oh, it is my lucky day - my lunch is coming to me.
After I eat my lunch, I am going to sleep.

Glen Morgan (10)
Ocklynge County Junior School, Eastbourne

The Minotaur

I wait till someone comes to find me
In this dark, damp and dismal place.
The smell of death on my breath
Just makes me hate myself.
I am half man, half bull.
I just want to be loved in any way by somebody.
I am in agony because I'm half starved.
I have to wait a year for someone to come down.

Jasmine Curtis-McFetters (11)
Ocklynge County Junior School, Eastbourne

The Minotaur

Here I am in my lair.
I wish I could be a real man.
I only have one friend, I think.
I lose count of the days and nights.
The walls are damp and the ceiling's low.
I wish I could be a real man.
I only really kill for food.
When people come, they're very rude.

Charlie Pearson (10)
Ocklynge County Junior School, Eastbourne

The Minotaur

I am the Minotaur,
I'm hating myself year by year.
I'm living in a dark, damp and dismal dungeon.
I have got to get BO with my venomous body.
Rotten saliva comes out of my disgusting mouth.
Every day I am waiting for my dreadful misery to end.
There's more places than home.
No Minotaur will have this life.

Jacob Adlam (10)
Ocklynge County Junior School, Eastbourne

The Minotaur

In the labyrinth's dark and gloomy passages,
I wait day and night for someone to come and find me
And put me out of my misery.
I live my days starved and misunderstood.
Feeding on mice is no way to live.
I see my sister once a year if I'm lucky,
It's not fair.
Aches and pains are all over me,
The smell of death on my breath,
There must be another way to live.
Oh, if someone knew just how it feels
To be left in here alone.
I am half man, half bull
And the pain is unimaginable.

Abigail Lain (10)
Ocklynge County Junior School, Eastbourne

The Minotaur

I'm the Minotaur, lonesome and bored.
I'm a weird creature,
I'm the weirdest creature in the world.
Even though my cell is freezing,
I drip with sweat.
I'm in pain - agony,
My neck and mouth fill me with anger
For my teeth don't fit my jaw properly
As they are the teeth of a lion.
My neck is straining and aching,
For my big bull's head is far too heavy for it.

No one in this cruel world is going to be my friend.

Alicia Pettit (10)
Ocklynge County Junior School, Eastbourne

The Minotaur

I am the wretched, self-hating Minotaur
Who wanders through the cold, damp cellar
Treading on the bones of victims
That I have had as meals over the past 14 years.

Every gloomy and starless night,
I lay here remembering the screams
And the faces of the poor people that I slaughtered
As if it were yesterday.

Every day I wander alone
In the never-ending maze of dread,
Listening to the sound of bone on stone
As I try to prevent my weighty horns
From dragging on the low, jagged ceiling.
My hooves feel as though they will fall off
Onto the floor of my filthy, smelly home.
My teeth are like cat and dog
Fighting to get comfortable.

Oh, how I wish I was human again.

Thomas Wardale (10)
Ocklynge County Junior School, Eastbourne

The Minotaur

I need a friend who will look after me,
I need to eat before I starve.
I need to tend my aching body
And I need to see the light of day.

My dungeon stinks of dry blood,
My dungeon is horrible.
My dungeon is my home,
But even so, I hate it.

Roya Arjomand (10)
Ocklynge County Junior School, Eastbourne

The Minotaur

I am the Minotaur, friendless and lonely.
I live in a dismal cellar, trapped like a prisoner.
All day I lie on the gloomy floor bored,
Picking human bones from my teeth.
Then, after seven years I feast on 14 humans,
Tearing at them.
There's no one to help me,
Who would, because I am the Minotaur.
I dream of light outside this jail,
Could I just have one week on bail?
No, of course not, I'm wretched aren't I?
Now I sit here, wanting to die.

Jack Williams (10)
Ocklynge County Junior School, Eastbourne

The Minotaur

When you look in my glowing, red eyes,
A rush of fear shoots down your body like roaring thunder.
I can see it in your eyes,
I can smell it on your breath.
If you come close enough,
You can feel the beat of my heart bellowing past you.
If you so much as feel my bolted, twisted, iron touch,
You would instantly be smashed into two forever and eternity.

Who am I?
Your worst nightmare - *The Minotaur!*

Matthew Khan (10)
Ocklynge County Junior School, Eastbourne

The Minotaur

I live in the labyrinth,
Terrified and lonely.
I hate it here, it's so dark and dismal.
I have no fun, I have no laughs
And I have no friends to talk to.
It's hard to be happy
In such a depressing, heart-wrenching dungeon.
I hate my life,
It's so miserable and meaningless.
I'm trapped and alone,
So I munch on flesh and I munch on bones,
But that just makes me worse.
My blade-sharp horns scratch the life out of people.
I live in pure agony, that's why I say
Don't feed me, kill me.

Courtney Dyer (10)
Ocklynge County Junior School, Eastbourne

The Minotaur

Why, oh why, do I live in this horrible, mossy, damp maze?
It took me about ten years to find my way around.
I hate the king who imprisoned me here.
Why can't I be outside amongst the people in the beautiful outside
world?
I rarely have any visitors and when I do, I eat them alive.
My ugly head is too heavy for my neck to support.
I can't sleep, I can't do anything.
Why am I like this?
Why am I like this?

Lewis Smith (10)
Ocklynge County Junior School, Eastbourne

Sounds At Park Gate

It was so quiet that I heard a magpie flapping its pretty wings.
It was so quiet that I heard my hair flying in the wind.
It was so quiet that I heard the bushes rustling in the quiet wind.
It was so quiet that I heard the gate swaying on its squeaky hinges.
It was so quiet that I heard the loud horns of cars in the distance.
It was so quiet that I heard the trees swaying around in the mad wind.
It was so quiet that I heard children writing their silent poems.

Anastasia Taylor (7)
Park Gate Primary School, Southampton

The Poetry Book's Pages

What do I see in the poetry book today?
I see such outstanding poems.

A Shakespearian character on an exquisite balcony,
A brave warrior with his bloody sword in hand,
A moonlit beach with a dancer on, I think
And a noble knight on his noble, trusty steed.

That's what I see in the poetry book today.

What do I hear in the poetry book today?
I hear such stupendous things.

A cry of a slain horse in a bloodstained battle,
A weary traveller dying with a terrible wound,
A black-hearted dragon rider, I think,
A cynical knight on his battle-weary steed.

That's what I hear in the poetry book today.

What do I feel in the poetry book today?
I feel such wholesome things.

A knight, happy on his victorious day,
A prince with his fair maiden, Lucy,
A bountiful knight on his good-hearted steed, I think
And an ecstatic man who's found true love.

That's what I feel in the poetry book today.

David Dumbleton (10)
Parkland J&I School, Eastbourne

What's It Like In Heaven?

What do I see in Heaven today?
I see such glistening things.

An angel with gleaming golden hair, sitting upon a unicorn,
A cherub with a fairy spirit playing on their lawn,
A gorgeous golden tabby cat walking up a path, I think,
And in the background, a splendid little cottage made of fresh,
glorious cream lilies (and pink!).

That's what I see in Heaven today.

What do I hear in Heaven today?
I hear such mystical things.

A string quartet on a raised, sheltered stage,
A sandy-coloured hamster squeaking, let out of its cage,
A dear little bunny rabbit, snuffling about in the grass, I think,
The scratching of a goose feather quill, writing in royal burgundy ink.

That's what I hear in Heaven today.

What do I feel in Heaven today?
I feel such amazing things.

A floaty, lilac silk ballgown on top of a flowing satin petticoat,
The extremely smooth water underneath this boat,
A rippling in the gentle breeze, I think,
And a thrill from the feeling of that handsome young boy's wink!

That's what I feel in Heaven today.

Laura Grant (10)
Parkland J&I School, Eastbourne

The Boy

There once was a boy who sat on our table,
Who sucked his thumb and his table,
Who loved jam tarts
And ate them with the Queen of Hearts,
That was the boy who sat on our table.

Alex Haywood (11)
Parkland J&I School, Eastbourne

Sweet Factory

What do I see in the sweet factory today?
I see such phenomenal things.

A strawberry-flavoured lace on a packet sealer,
A packet of sherbet lemons with sherbet lollies,
A strange-looking chocolate bar shaped like a gun, I think,
A packet of chocolate éclairs on a conveyor belt moving slowly
                                    to a packet sealer.

That's what I see in the sweet factory today.

What do I hear in the sweet factory today?
I hear some peculiar things.

I hear a machine stamping on packets of Snickers,
I hear a conveyor belt moving with a slow pace,
I hear sweets being made on the other side of the factory, I think,
I hear loads of packets creasing and being picked up by machinery.

That's what I hear in the sweet factory today.

What do I feel in the sweet factory today?
I feel such exceptional things.

I feel an amazing feeling in part of my stomach,
Because of the smell of chocolate and sweets.
I feel a chocolate bar in my mouth with a caramel centre,
I feel that I should eat all the sweets, but they will notice I think,
I feel a sweet in my chocolatey fingers and the sugar trickling out
                                    of my fingers.

That's what I feel in the sweet factory today.

Joshua Rank (10)
Parkland J&I School, Eastbourne

The Coral Reef

What do I see in the coral reef today?
I see such kaleidoscopic things.
Lots of tincture on coral creatures,
A razor-sharp fanged sea serpent with an electrical sting, I think,
A coral creature with an exquisite procedure for catching
helpless fish,
That's what I see in the coral reef today.

What do I hear in the coral reef today?
I hear such composed things.
An octopus struggling onto a rock,
A crab with fidgety snippers,
A whale's screeching from a distance, I think,
The crashing of waves above me,
That's what I hear in the coral reef today.

What do I feel in the coral reef today?
I feel such sensational things.
The oozing sand on my saturated feet,
A school of fish with silky scales,
A slimy bunch of seaweed, I think,
The painfulness of a rock against my helpless foot,
That's what I feel in the coral reef today.

Timothy Carr (10)
Parkland J&I School, Eastbourne

The Teddy

It's as blue as the ocean,
It sounds like an elephant,
It feels soft and comfy,
It looks like a blue whale,
It smells like rotten fish,
It tastes like sweet potatoes,
It reminds me of a fishing boat.

Elliott Field (10)
Parkland J&I School, Eastbourne

Stars

What do I see in the stars today?
I see such phenomenal things.
A princess with golden locks in her hair
On a white, wispy-maned unicorn with such twinkling blue eyes,
A dazzling ball gown fit for a queen
With criss-cross stars embroidered onto the long, flowing gown,
A gynormous mint choc chip, six scoop ice cream with seven flakes,
I think,
A crown with rubies and emeralds on the top of the points.

That's what I see in the stars today.

What do I hear in the stars today?
I hear such tremendous things.
An extremely quiet whisper from the stars saying echo, echo,
A middlish sound of a cool breeze rushing past the sky.

That's what I hear in the stars today.

What do I feel in the stars today?
I feel such funny things.
A cold feeling rushing through my blood, veins and body,
I feel nothing else from the stars today.

Kelsey McCann (10)
Parkland J&I School, Eastbourne

Excited

Excited is the colour blue
Excited is the sounds of TV
Excited feels like a bungee jump
Excited looks like a bouncy castle
Excited smells like fresh mints
Excited tastes like my tasty chips
Excited reminds me of my bestest friend - Grace.

Natasha Cameron (10)
Parkland J&I School, Eastbourne

Sparkling Loch

What do I see in the sparkling loch tonight?
I see such artistic things.

A lunging seagull in the glinting sky,
A Loch Ness monster with gliding scales,
A flying fish is flying through the gleaming air, I think,
A dolphin is screeching high enough to shatter glass.

That's what I see on the sparkling loch tonight.

What do I hear in the sparkling loch tonight?
I hear such glorious things.

A wave plunging on the jagged rocks,
A beautiful mermaid with a thrashing tail,
A scavenging badger lurking around the loch,
An owl drifting across the moonlit sky.

That's what I hear in the sparkling loch tonight.

Declan Gee (10)
Parkland J&I School, Eastbourne

Holidays

Holidays are fun,
Holidays are cool,
Holidays are great,
Everyone goes!
Holidays in the sun,
Holidays in the cold,
Everyone enjoys!
Holidays in a caravan,
Holidays in a tent,
Holidays everywhere!
Holidays in Scotland,
Holidays in the USA,
Holidays are fun,
Holidays are cool,
Holidays are just . . . *great!*

Jessica Capon (9)
Parkland J&I School, Eastbourne

The Meadow

What do I see in the meadow today?
I see such remarkable things.

A fluffy lamb on top of a mountain of mud,
A remarkable buttercup opening into a wonderful flower,
A spotted toadstool where fairies live, I think,
A beautiful butterfly fluttering around near the tum-tum tree.

That's what I see in the meadow today.

What do I hear in the meadow today?
I hear such amazing things.

A lovely bird looking after its baby,
The wet, long grass covered in dew,
A frog burping on me, I think,
A rabbit nibbling at a carrot from the farmer's field next door.

That's what I hear in the meadow today.

Victoria Baldwin (10)
Parkland J&I School, Eastbourne

A Colourful World

A colourful bird in the sky swooping down,
A picture of a chubby worm floating in the sky,
A sunset shining on the rippling water,
A boat floating in the water and fish swimming in the sea.

That is what I see in the sea today.

What do I hear in the sea today?
I hear the waves splashing against the shore,
A fish in and out of the beautiful sea,
A dolphin splashing in and out with its fins waggling behind it,
A boat with a man shouting as it sinks.

Natalie Healey & Tamar Hawkins (10)
Parkland J&I School, Eastbourne

Chocolate Shop

What do I see in the chocolate shop today?
I see such scrumptious things.

A massive bar of chocolate on the big desk,
A chocolate bar with icing on top and treacle toffee in the middle,
Aero and some chocolate Flakes, I think,
Five Snicker bars have been sold.

That's what I see in the chocolate shop today.

What do I hear in the chocolate shop today?
I hear such loud people talking about chocolate.

A loud till on the desk,
A loud machine with chocolate wrappers coming out,
A lorry filled with chocolate just pulled up, I think,
Boxes of Aero have been brought in.

That's what I hear in the chocolate shop today.

Michael Shefford (10)
Parkland J&I School, Eastbourne

Kennings

Furniture scratcher,
Mouse catcher.

Water hater,
Bird chaser.

Soft fur,
Likes to purr.

Loves food,
Soppy mood.

What am I?

Sophie Wormald (10)
Parkland J&I School, Eastbourne

Animals - Kennings

Finger pincher,
Fire spitter,
Body squeezer,
Heat seeker,
Poison ejector,
Light lover,
Pollen sucker,
Humming flier,
Annoying bug,
Scaley swimmer,
Beautiful flier,
Monstrous beast,
Spotted runner,
Beast king,
Man's friend,
Smelling hunter,
Stinky mammal.

Alistair Home (10)
Parkland J&I School, Eastbourne

A Tiger Kenning

Clever hunter
Stripy punter

Fast runner
Bone crusher

Quick killer
Loves dinner.

What am I?

Stephanie Hellier (11)
Parkland J&I School, Eastbourne

The Seaside!

What do I see at the seaside today?
I see such scrumptious things.

A shell on the bright yellow sand,
A crab with eight long legs.

A dazzling blue dolphin, I think,
A starfish with glittery, pink skin.

That's what I see at the seaside today.

What do I hear at the seaside today?
I hear such wonderful things.

A bright purple butterfly on the sand fluttering away,
A beautiful fish with shiny scales glowing away.

A whale as grey as the sky on a winter's day,
A grey whale wandering around in the sea, as slow as a snail,
I think.

That's what I hear at the seaside today.

Megan Prangnell Montieth (10)
Parkland J&I School, Eastbourne

South Downs

What do I see on the Downs today?
I see such prettyful things.
A fuzzy rabbit on a garland of flowers,
A phenomenal mole with pride and glory,
A cat with blood all around its mouth, I think,
A handful of worms digging in the earth.
That's what I see on the Downs today.

Ellen Mathias-Bevan (10)
Parkland J&I School, Eastbourne

The Note

John passed a note to Joe.
'What's going on? I want to know.'
'It's none of your business, so turn around.'

But nobody noticed that there,
Sitting on her chair, was teacher.

The note passed from front to back,
First to Mary, then to Jack.

But nobody noticed that there,
Sitting on her chair, was teacher.

The class began to giggle,
The silent note had reached the middle.

The joke was spreading all around,
No one can hear the deadly sound.

But nobody noticed that there,
Sitting on her . . . *oh no! She's behind you!*

Lloyd Thursfield (10)
Parkland J&I School, Eastbourne

Stupid

Stupid is as green as grass,
It sounds like someone in pain,
It feels like a scared cat,
It looks like a bat,
It smells like rotten food,
It tastes like sick,
It reminds me of my hamster.

Christopher Blackman (10)
Parkland J&I School, Eastbourne

The Forest

What do I see in the enchanted forest today?
I see such magical things.
A crazy monkey on an everlasting banana tree,
A parrot with rainbow-coloured feathers,
A fresh sky with fluffy, ice-white clouds, I think,
A pair of crocodiles in the shallows of the muddy river,
That's what I see in the glorious forest today.

What do I hear in the tropical forest today?
I hear such unusual things.
A blow of the sweet fruit-smelling air on the thick branches,
A sound of beautiful birds with eyes as blue as the sea,
A herd of many elephants having a swim in the river, I think,
A gathering of tigers finding something to eat,
That's what I hear in the wonderful forest today.

What do I feel in the beautiful forest today?
I feel such extraordinary things.
A patch of long grass tickling my legs,
A warm breeze on my cheek with a cold breeze on the other cheek,
A feeling of a free, explorable feeling, I think,
It's a feeling I will never forget!
That's what I feel in the unforgettable forest today.

Pia Jackson (10)
Parkland J&I School, Eastbourne

Creepy-Crawlie Creatures

What do I see on the dry bank today?
I see such fabulous things.
A spiky hedgehog on a green leaf,
A brightly coloured bird with a wiggly worm,
A dark brown bird's nest, I think,
A berry bramble bush,
That's what I see on the dry bank today.

What do I hear on the dry bank today?
I hear such noisy things.
A beautiful barn owl on a thin twig,
The wind rustling the bright green leaves,
A blackbird singing, I think,
A pile of swooping autumn-coloured leaves,
That's what I hear on the dry bank today.

What do I feel on the dry bank today?
I feel such slimy things.
A slippery snail on a little thorn,
A ladybird with a creepy-crawlie spider,
A rough, black woodlouse, I think,
A sneaky, sly bunny rabbit,
That's what I feel on the dry bank today.

Beth Adams (10)
Parkland J&I School, Eastbourne

Seashells, Seashells!

What do I see in the seashells today?
I see such marvellous things.
A man who's just like me on a stack of shiny money,
A millionaire with a car made of golden, sweet chocolate,
A magical genie who grants as many wishes as you want,
A money-making turkey that can make millions of pounds.
That's what I see in the seashells today.

What do I hear in the calm air tonight?
I hear such strange things.
A clam singing a song upon the swarthy waves,
Another clam singing a song with the two pearls in her mouth,
A woman wishing to get a speedboat, I think,
A child waiting to get attention.
That's what I hear in the calm air tonight.

What do I feel in the hot sand today?
I feel such unbelievable things.
A fairy with stacks of gold sitting on a rock of wonders,
An angel with glittery wings that twinkle in the sun,
A prince trying to find his true love, I think,
A princess who's found her true love.
That's what I feel in the hot sand today.

Dan Waters (10)
Parkland J&I School, Eastbourne

The Wind

The wind is a kitten chasing the leaves around my house,
Playfully running round in circles pouncing on them.

The wind is an eagle swooping through my house,
Golden colours flashing around me.

The wind is a butterfly fluttering around my house,
With beautiful colours on his wings, he taps on the windowpane.

Chloe Ralphs (10)
Peter Gladwin Primary School, Portslade

Our Street

Number 7 is a middle-class, robust man,
Living his city life,
Looking down at his smaller neighbours,
Surveying his open grounds.

Numbers 9 and 11 are alter ego,
An old, friendly fellow,
Or the grumpy madman who hates everyone down the road,
Never knowing where one ends and the other begins.

Number 13 is a tallish, dull, middle-aged man,
He is shy and frightened of the outside world,
He's unlucky, tired and secretive,
Sick of people having a good old peek into his soul.

Number 15 is a lonely, elderly lady,
She was orphaned at a young age,
Now she has no one to care for her,
Crumbling away, she will eventually be gone.

Timmy Dunkerton (11)
Peter Gladwin Primary School, Portslade

The Wind

The wind is a furious lion,
Prowling around my house,
Moaning and swishing her tail violently.

The wind is a playful puppy,
Rushing around outside my house,
Barking excitedly and wagging his tail,
Scratching at the door, trying to get in.

The wind is a sparrow,
Gliding gracefully around my house,
Singing her song as she passes by,
But her friendly voice soon fades away.

Ione Gamble (10)
Peter Gladwin Primary School, Portslade

Our Street

Number 7 is a nosey young man,
He overlooks his neighbours,
Rich and in possession of lots of cars,
Always busy in the city.

Numbers 9 and 11 are alter ego twins,
9 is nice and comforting,
11 is nasty and doesn't like people,
Despite this, they get on well.

Number 13 is an unlucky man,
Tired, quiet and secretive,
Afraid to go outside
And no one to turn to.

Number 15 is lonely and uncared for,
Has no friend to talk to,
Slowly, painfully dying,
Minutes to the grave.

Aaron Brace (11)
Peter Gladwin Primary School, Portslade

The Wind

The wind is a hawk swooping around my house at supersonic speed
And tearing everything off its hinges
Whilst diving around to catch its prey
Its wings darken the sky.

The wind is a rhino, large and imposing,
Trampling and demolishing, shattering and battering
Wherever it goes it devastates my house
Within seconds the roof starts to close in on itself.

The wind is a monkey swinging through my window
Swirling, suspended from the broken pipes
And whistling a classical melody
Humming between the cracks and crevices of the broken wall.

Matthew Grant (10)
Peter Gladwin Primary School, Portslade

Our Street

Number 7 is a muscular man,
With his nose pointed high,
Looking down on his neighbours rudely,
He's very fortunate and smart.

Numbers 9 and 11 are alter ego,
Fun and outgoing, sad and shy,
Hopefully these two personalities will never mix,
Thankfully, they never will.

Number 13 is a lonely, uncomforted, shy girl,
Tall, thin and extremely fragile,
An orphan, tired and secretive,
Dull and terrified, in need of some serious attention.

Number 15 is an elderly woman,
Uncared for, depressed and extremely ill,
Alone and afraid, tortured by her illness,
Soon enough her suffering will be over.

Paige Wickens (10)
Peter Gladwin Primary School, Portslade

Our Street

Numbers 9 and 11 are identical twins,
Sharing their secrets,
Always looking their best,
Never arguing.

Number 13 is a frightened man,
Standing in the darkness,
Lonely as can be,
Until the return of the light.

Number 15 is for sale,
Neglected and sad,
No window boxes,
The owner feels bad.

Bryony Reynolds (10)
Peter Gladwin Primary School, Portslade

What Type Of House Are You?

Number 7 is a wealthy youth,
He's tall and smart,
Always rushing around,
Ignoring his neighbours as he goes.

Numbers 9 and 11 are identical twin sisters,
Sharing their ideas and secrets,
With their Gucci handbags and Prada clothes,
They're the mirror image of each other.

Number 13 is a tall and jolly woman,
But not the brightest of people.
She can be quite shy and frightened of other people,
An extremely unlucky person.

Number 15 is an elderly man,
With no one to care for or look after him.
He's lonely, with a terrible illness,
He feels there is no reason to carry on.

George Dunkerton (11)
Peter Gladwin Primary School, Portslade

The Wind

The wind is a soaring eagle
Tearing on my window
Looping, hoping and swooping
Shaking the house until it falls.

The wind is a jumping bunny
Bouncing and pouncing
Lolloping and leaping joyfully
Being as happy as she could be.

The wind is a silent tiger
Ready to catch what he finds
Off he goes, speeding and whizzing away
Tearing apart his helpless prey.

Isi Fink (10)
Peter Gladwin Primary School, Portslade

Our Street

Number 7 is a muscular young man,
With sparkling, shiny eyes,
He is smart and statuesque
And very lucky.

Numbers 9 and 11 are identical twins,
They are tall and thin,
Smart and bold,
They share each other's secrets.

Number 13 is a dull lady,
She is shy and glum,
She is tall and thin,
She is unlucky and very fatigued.

Number 15 is a lonely man,
He is uncared for,
He is short and stout,
He is dirty and grubby.

Darcey Clark (10)
Peter Gladwin Primary School, Portslade

Our Street

Number 7 is a powerful man with strong, twinkling eyes,
He is rich and drives posh cars
And isn't horrible to his friends.

Numbers 9 and 11 are best friends who are sharing secrets
And never break friendship.
They have the same hobby.

Number 13 is a tall, thin person who is a bit shy,
But sometimes he goes out into the big city.
His only friend is his dog, Tom.

Number 15 is a poor little woman,
She has no one to talk to and all she hears is silence.
Her friend is the little woman down the road.

Sam Ralphs (10)
Peter Gladwin Primary School, Portslade

Our Street

Number 7 is an elevated young man,
With a sneaky personality,
Wearing a top of the range suit
With a Taz tie.

Numbers 9 and 11 are identical twins,
They both have sparkling eyes, but have grubby faces.
They like getting into trouble and being filthy
And their clothes are always the same.

Number 13 is a secretive woman with little personality,
She never speaks and her eyes remain closed.
She hides away from the world,
She will always stay the same.

Number 15 is a lovely old woman,
With no one to care for her.
She tries to make friends,
But the days slip by.

Sam Talbot (10)
Peter Gladwin Primary School, Portslade

The Wind

The wind is a mad baboon,
Biting my fingers,
Snatching and rampaging
Around my house.

The wind is a herd of rogue elephants,
Stampeding across my living room,
Crushing everything in their path,
Sitting on me.

The wind is an African wild dog,
Biting and crushing fiercely,
Chasing, slashing and hunting cows.

Daniel Hart (11)
Peter Gladwin Primary School, Portslade

Our Street

Number 7 is an elevated, rich, juvenile woman,
Who likes everything to be immaculate.
7 is her lucky number
And she is very, very sneaky.

Numbers 9 and 11 are identical twins,
They are always playing together.
They love music and getting filthy,
Their favourite thing is getting into trouble.

Number 13 is surreptitious and demure,
She is always tired and she loves her bed.
She likes being alone
And she is very unlucky.

Number 15 is an ill old lady,
She wishes to get better.
Some days she feels healthy,
But she knows there is no cure.

Rebekah Strong (10)
Peter Gladwin Primary School, Portslade

The Wind

The wind is a panther racing towards my mansion,
Blowing the roof off and the door off its hinges.

The wind is a mouse rushing through the leaves,
Stopping for a minute, then rushing out again.

The wind takes flight, it hovers around the sky and trees,
Ever tweeting, ever whistling, the wind is a bird that takes flight.

Sarah Green (10)
Peter Gladwin Primary School, Portslade

My Street

Number 7 is a wealthy woman who
Is very tall and young
She is a business woman
Who is very bright.

Numbers 9 and 11 are identical twins
With golden hair and pierced ears
They look the same.
Sharing secrets and reading books
They enjoy being together
Making cakes is their favourite hobby.

Number 13 is a boring, shy person
Who never comes out.
She lacks intelligence
She is unlucky.

Number 15 is a depressed man
Who only wants a family to care for.
His illness is getting worse
Soon he will be gone.

Katie Lillywhite (10)
Peter Gladwin Primary School, Portslade

Our Street

Number 7 is a husky man,
He's grand, lean and upper class,
Looking down at his neighbours,
He is a prosperous estate agent.

Numbers 9 and 11 are alter egos,
By day he is a normal old man,
By night he's an RAF pilot,
Teaching students how to fly fighter jets.

Number 13 is an unlucky old lady,
She is tired, secretive, shy and frightened,
She rarely leaves her house,
She is thin and ill and scared of the outside world.

Number 15 is an orphan,
With nobody to care for him,
Lonely and scared with only rats and spiders for comfort,
Alone in the world with nothing to keep him warm
In the winter months.

Ben Ffitch (10)
Peter Gladwin Primary School, Portslade

The Wind

The wind is a bear
Galloping through my hall
The wind is a bear
Scratching at my cupboards
The wind is a bear
Growling at my window
The wind is a bear
Ripping through my pillow.

The wind is a wolf
Howling in my hall
The wind is a wolf
Scratching at my door
The wind is a wolf
Chasing my shadow
The wind is a wolf
Growling at my bedroom door.

The wind is an owl
Flying at supersonic speed
The wind is an owl
Glaring at my window
The wind is an owl
Hooting in my ear
The wind is an owl
Watching me all the time.

Stefen Chapman (10)
Peter Gladwin Primary School, Portslade

Our Street

Number 7 is a young, rich, slim lady,
With posh, new, gleaming clothes.
She likes to keep things immaculate
And enjoys her privacy.

Numbers 9 and 11 are identical twins.
They are smartly dressed
And like to keep things perfect.
They have great personalities.

Number 13 is a tired, unlucky, thin lady.
She is very lonely with no one to look after her.
She is dull, with no money to spend as she has got no job.
She is too lacklustre to work.

Number 15 is a small, wide, lonely old man,
With no one to care for him.
No one notices him and he is wasting away.
Soon he is going to die.

Georgia Cronin (10)
Peter Gladwin Primary School, Portslade

I Am

I am a black panther chasing a zebra in the long grass.
I am a cat's bed made from fur and wool sitting in a shop window
                                    waiting to be bought.
I am the moon and stars shining down on all the land.

I am a big, red, shiny and juicy apple sitting in a fruit bowl
                                    waiting to be eaten.
I am a pair of blue, flarey jeans scraping across the ground.
I am a Victorian mansion with ghosts haunting my walls.
I am a scream blasting from a fairground ride.

Claudia Cole (10)
Portfield Community Primary School, Chichester

I Am Waiting

I am a fluffy, white kitten sitting outside my house
Waiting for my owner to come back and feed me my food.

I am a sofa in the shape of lips.
I am bright red and waiting for you to come and sit on me.

I am the scalding sunshine shining in the sky
Burning you away.

I am a chicken waiting to be carved
For dinner.

I am a pair of black boots standing on the floor
Waiting for you to put me on.

I am a church in town with people surrounding me
Waiting for the bride to come out.

I am a piano playing the most wonderful tune ever
And I am in the middle of nowhere.

Shanice Wilson (10)
Portfield Community Primary School, Chichester

I Am A . . .

I am a sabre-toothed tiger.

I am in Alaska.

I am a coat hanger being useful.

I am a thundercloud that strikes fear into the hearts
of all who see me.

I am a pepperoni pizza and a rhubarb crumble and custard.

I am a pair of trousers on a stall.

I am a skyscraper in London.

I am the song of love.

Ryan Ellis (11)
Portfield Community Primary School, Chichester

What Am I?

I am bear in my cave
I am sleeping just after fighting
I am dreaming of being with someone

I am an old sofa in a shop
I am sat on by loads of people
I am never bought though

I am a hurricane heading towards the USA
I am going to knock things over
I am going really fast

I am a chocolate fudge cake
I am going to be eaten by the ten-year-old
I am going to have fun

I am a pair of socks
I am in Marks and Spencers
I am behind millions of other socks

I am a huge skyscraper
I am in New York City
I am an office for many people

I am a roar of a lion
I am used a lot
I am going to run out soon.

Dominic Mortimer (10)
Portfield Community Primary School, Chichester

My Dreams

I am a fish searching the Great Barrier Reef for food for my young.

I am an old, black, Chinese tea table.

I am a tiny raindrop dripping from the sky.

I am a sausage walking down the beach.

I am a Spanish red dress waiting to dance.

I am an old Tudor cottage in Scotland.

I am a vibration of a band's drum.

Rachael Ambler (10)
Portfield Community Primary School, Chichester

When I Was One

When I was one,
I made a bun.

When I was two,
I made a shoe.

When I was three,
I fell out of the tree.

When I was four,
I was poor.

When I was five,
I was alive.

When I was six,
I ate Twix.

When I was seven,
I was in Devon.

Esther Akehurst (6)
Rotherfield Primary School, Crowborough

When I Was One

When I was one,
I sucked my thumb.
When I was two,
I walked into a zoo.
When I was three,
I was pulled out of a tree.
When I was four,
I always snored.
When I was five,
I sat on a beehive.
When I was six,
I dropped a brick.
When I was seven,
I went to Devon.
When I was eight,
I touched a snake.

Oliver Pilbeam (8)
Rotherfield Primary School, Crowborough

Louder Than A Clap Of Thunder

Louder than a clap of thunder,
That's really loud.
Louder than a big werewolf that howled.
Louder than a big, black bomb,
That would take really long.
Louder than a plane shooting fire.
Your dad doesn't snore.
Ann Pope's such a liar.
Louder than a clap of thunder,
That's how loud my father snores!

Mirran Harper (7)
Rotherfield Primary School, Crowborough

When I Was One

When I was one,
I ate a bun.

When I was two,
I threw my shoe.

When I was three,
I won a trophy.

When I was four,
I got locked in a door.

When I was five,
I could dive.

When I was six,
I could mix.

When I was seven,
I went to Heaven.

Sam Osborne (7)
Rotherfield Primary School, Crowborough

When I Was One

When I was one,
I lost my thumb.

When I was two,
I lost my zoo.

When I was three,
I had a gold key.

When I was four,
I blocked the door.

When I was five,
I was not alive.

When I was six,
I could play tricks.

Harry Chittenden (6)
Rotherfield Primary School, Crowborough

When I Was One

When I was one,
I loved my mum.

When I was two,
I lost my new shoe.

When I was three,
I lost my new key.

When I was four,
I got locked in a door.

When I was five,
I went near a beehive.

When I was six,
I ate a Twix.

When I was seven,
I went to Devon.

When I was eight,
I had my first mate.

Holly Jenkins (6)
Rotherfield Primary School, Crowborough

Wintertime

W inter is a happy time when the snow is dropping.
 I love snowmen when they are flopping.
N o, don't go!
T o melt in the snow.
E very spring the snow goes away.
R emembering a sad day.

James Miller (7)
Rotherfield Primary School, Crowborough

When I Was One

When I was one,
I sat on a gun.

When I was two,
I was nearly new.

When I was three,
I was hardly me.

When I was four,
I was nearly poor.

When I was five,
I lived in a hive.

When I was six,
I did some tricks.

When I was seven,
I went to Heaven
And did not come back
To be eleven.

Lucy Evans (7)
Rotherfield Primary School, Crowborough

Red Is Like . . .

Red is like the setting sun
Yellow is like a field of corn
Green is like a jumping frog
Blue is like the ocean deep
Orange is like a bonfire burning bright
Purple is like round, juicy plums
Brown is like wet, sticky mud.

Brooke Steadman (6)
Rotherfield Primary School, Crowborough

When I Was One

When I was one,
I had fun.

When I was two,
I ate baby goo.

When I was three,
I played with trees.

When I was four,
I was stuck in the door.

When I was five,
I learnt to dive.

When I was six,
I ate some sticks.

When I was seven,
I liked Heaven.

Hannah Russell (8)
Rotherfield Primary School, Crowborough

Autumn Days

September is an autumn month,
The leaves start falling down,
They make a beautiful crown.

The acorn has a little hat,
When the wind blows, it falls down flat,
Badgers make their cosy beds.
        Autumn!

Katy Jackson (7)
Rotherfield Primary School, Crowborough

When I Was One

When I was one,
I ate a bun.

When I was two,
I got stuck with glue.

When I was three,
I got a key.

When I was four,
I shut my finger in the door.

When I was five,
I learnt to dive.

When I was six,
I played some tricks.

When I was seven,
I nearly went to Heaven.

Denver Weller-Tomsett (7)
Rotherfield Primary School, Crowborough

When I Was One

When I was one,
I ate a bun.

When I was two,
I was blue.

When I was three,
I could write poetry.

When I was four,
I had a war.

When I was five,
I could drive.

When I was six,
I had a friend who could do a trick.

Arthur William Walker (7)
Rotherfield Primary School, Crowborough

When I Was One

When I was one,
I sucked my thumb.

When I was two,
I lost a shoe.

When I was three,
I ran away to sea.

When I was four,
I shut the door.

When I was five,
I touched a hive.

When I was six,
I had some tricks.

When I was seven,
I went to Devon.

Olivia Charles (7)
Rotherfield Primary School, Crowborough

I Saw

I saw a pig fight a whale,
I saw a zombie ringing a bell,
I saw a skeleton break the door,
I saw a baby eat the moon,
I saw a tortoise eat a whale,
I saw my dad sleeping next to a rat,
I saw rats having a war,
I saw ants making others walkers,
I saw a bat smack a cat,
I saw a cat whack a mat.

Robert Allison (7)
Rotherfield Primary School, Crowborough

When I Was One

When I was one,
It was fun.

When I was two,
My favourite colour was blue.

When I was three,
I ate my tea.

When I was four,
I slammed the door.

When I was five,
I felt alive.

When I was six,
I could do some tricks.

When I was seven,
I went to Devon.

When I was eight,
I had lots of mates.

Sophie-Rose McDonagh (7)
Rotherfield Primary School, Crowborough

I Asked The Little Boy Who Cannot See

Red is like the strong roar of a lion.
Yellow is like the soft feel of a banana.
Green is like the quiet rustle of the leaves.
Blue is like the powerful breeze of wind.
Orange is like the sweet scent of marmalade.
Purple is like the raging thunder.
Brown is like the warm taste of chocolate.

Max Bates (7)
Rotherfield Primary School, Crowborough

When I Was One

When I was one,
I ate a bun.

When I was two,
I went to the zoo.

When I was three,
I went to sea.

When I was four,
I sat by the door.

When I was five,
I had a drive.

When I was six,
I picked up sticks.

When I was seven,
I went to Devon.

Amy Dodd (7)
Rotherfield Primary School, Crowborough

Autumn Time

Acorns fall from the tree
Because squirrels are looking for their tea
And in the chestnut tree
There are some conkers.

Fergus Wilson (7)
Rotherfield Primary School, Crowborough

When I Was One

When I was one,
I lost my mum.

When I was two,
I lost a shoe.

When I was three,
I won a trophy.

When I was four,
I broke the law.

When I was five,
I was hardly alive.

When I was six,
I was a mix.

When I was seven,
I died and went to Heaven.

Nathan Dewhurst (6)
Rotherfield Primary School, Crowborough

I Sat

I sat on a green mat.
I sat on a black bat.
I sat on a golden cat.
I sat on a smelly cowpat.
I sat on a blood-eating gnat.
I sat on a golden plait.
I sat on a golden hat.
I'm very clumsy to sit on all those things.

Sophie Gray (7)
Rotherfield Primary School, Crowborough

When I Was One

When I was one,
I looked at a fat bun.

When I was two,
I ate my dad's shoe.

When I was three,
I got pushed into a tree.

When I was four,
I got stuck in a door.

When I was five,
I hit a beehive.

When I was six,
I ate Weetabix and a Twix.

When I was seven,
I went to Heaven.

When I was eight,
I got stuck in a gate.

Jake Tibbutt (8)
Rotherfield Primary School, Crowborough

The Spider's Letter

(Poem in the style of Tony Diterlizzi - 'The Spider and the Fly')

The spider wrote a letter,
A letter of love, it seemed,
But when you read it better,
It was for different means.

It began with 'Dear Miss Fly,
I have seen you in the sky,
With your pale gossamer wings,
And your delicate fingers and rings.
Your poetry is delightful,
And, though you find me frightful,
I would like you to drop in
Because it is not a sin
To call upon your admirers,
For of seeing you I am tireless'.

And he carried on with this flattery,
Till his lamp ran low on its battery.
But at the end were the words
That most spiders would find absurd,
'Miss Fly, I miss you dearly,'
Then he wrote, 'From yours sincerely'.

And the last of his strength then did enable
Him to go and set the table.

Very soon the young Miss Fly
Came slowly and daintily fluttering by,
But as soon as she was inside, her
Body was dinner for the crafty spider.

And the sneaky spider felt no remorse,
As he greedily ate his second course.

Laura Willis (10)
St Giles CE Primary School, Horsted Keynes

The Reader Of This Poem

(Inspired by 'The Writer of this Poem' by Roger McGough)

The reader of this poem
Is as cracked as a nut,
As daft as a treacle toffee
As mucky as a mutt.

As troublesome as bubblegum
As brash as a Year 11,
As bouncy as a cheerful hum
As quiet as in Heaven.

As sneaky as a rat
As tappy toe as jazz,
As empty as an empty hat
As echoey as as as as
As as as . . .

As bossy as a whistle
As prickly as pins and a needle,
Of boots made out of thistles
And believe me it's not feeble!

As vain as trainers
As boring as a room,
As smelly as a drain is
Outside in the gloom.

Alfie Goldsmith (10)
St Margaret's CE Primary School, Ditchling

The Reader Of This Poem

(Inspired by 'The Writer of this Poem' by Roger McGough)

The reader of this poem,
Is as fat as a fat cat,
As mushy as a banana,
As flat as a mat that's been squashed by a fat cat!

George Waring (10)
St Margaret's CE Primary School, Ditchling

The Animal Kingdom

The elephants are louder than a thunderstorm
Through the grass.
The cheetahs run as fast as a train
That flies right past.

The eagles fly just like a plane
They still have time to play.
The owl can turn its head around
So he can look out for his prey.

The camel's got two humps or one
He lives in a beautiful bay.
The kangaroos are red or brown
They're always saying g-day.

Georgina Marshall (9)
St Margaret's CE Primary School, Ditchling

The Reader Of This Poem

(Inspired by 'The Writer of this Poem' by Roger McGough)

The reader of this poem
Is as slow as a snail
As graceful as a swan
As sharp as a nail

As cunning as a fox
As delicate as a plate
As still as a cardboard box
As lifeless as some slate

As fat as a lazy cat
As boring as a log
As sneaky as a flying bat
As sleepy as a dog.

Scarlett Pickup (10)
St Margaret's CE Primary School, Ditchling

The Reader Of This Poem

(Inspired by 'The Writer of this Poem' by Roger McGough)

The reader of this poem
Is as funky as jazz
As smelly as dirty washing
As funny as my mate, Baz.

As silly as a clown
As musical as pop
As green as the Downs
As high as the top.

As cold as ice
As wet as rain
As dotty as dice
As stuffy as a train.

As soft as a kitten
As hard as a wall
As woolly as a mitten
As colourful as the mall.

Nicola Bowman (9)
St Margaret's CE Primary School, Ditchling

The Newcomer

'There's something new in the jungle,'
Tiger said as it prowled,
'It's got no stripes, no sound, no appetite,
and not even a growl.'

Luke Buckman (8)
St Margaret's CE Primary School, Ditchling

The Reader Of This Poem

(Inspired by 'The Writer of this Poem' by Roger McGough)

The reader of this poem,
Is as bony as a pony,
As daft as a laugh,
As sick as macaroni.

As black as a boot,
A laugh like splintered thorns,
Worth as much as stolen loot
And ears which look like horns.

As lazy as a cow,
As bossy as Sven,
Whose favourite sound is miaow,
And clucks like a hen.

As smelly as a sock,
As fast as Owen,
As silent as a doe
Is the reader of this poem!

Ben Rudling (10)
St Margaret's CE Primary School, Ditchling

Sneaky

As sneaky as a burglar climbing through a windowpane,
As quiet as a cat,
As disgusting as a gurgly drain,
As snuggly as a hat.

As calm as a kite,
As it flies up in the sky,
So rough as a midday flight
But I watch my kite fly by.

Rebecca Bennis (9)
St Margaret's CE Primary School, Ditchling

He Swaggers Along

He swaggers along,
He thinks he's hard,
He acts like he's tough,
But inside he is as soft as a cushion.

He looks at his friends,
All laughing and joking,
He's as scared as a mouse,
But he won't admit it.

He'd like to be cool,
But he feels like he's not,
He'd like to be home,
All warm by the fire.

Through the cat flap - home at last!

Hannah Skinner & George Greenstreet (10)
St Margaret's CE Primary School, Ditchling

The Old Fish

There was an old fish who lived in a dish,
He owned an axe and liked to swish.
The old fish swims in the seas,
His favourite food is smelly goat's cheese.

Then one day the fish got ill,
He fell out of the dish on the window sill.
Three days later the old fish dies,
Though it wasn't a big surprise.

Jamie Beveridge (9)
St Margaret's CE Primary School, Ditchling

The Eagle

Soaring as silent as the night, taking its toll,
I have a keen eye for searching out my prey,
I have a knack for speed, diving from cliffs,
My wings save my soul.

Sam Sanders (10)
St Margaret's CE Primary School, Ditchling

Anger

An ox is angry, charging for its prey to kill,
The taste is bitter, gritty, hot, hard and bubbly.
The sound of screeching, screaming,
A quiet sound, spooky and haunting, silent but threatening.
It smells like burning cigarette smoke rising up to the sky . . .
I smell anger.

Alex Blowey (9)
St Mark's CE Primary School, Hadlow Down

Poem Of Anger

Anger feels spiky and hard all over,
The smell of burning wood is horrible,
The taste is the worst - it sticks in your mouth,
The colour is a red-pink, like fire in your house,
The sound is horrible nails scratching on the blackboard,
It seems like a biting crocodile eating my toes.

Katie Lee (9)
St Mark's CE Primary School, Hadlow Down

Wish I Were Gone

I'm alone and small, jealous too,
The words in my throat tasting
Like smoke . . .
I hate you.

Anger's hands on my face,
Burning hot, yet ice-cold,
Like shattered glass on my face,
Growing on me like mould.

Jealousy's reaching my heart,
Clenching my insides,
I'm so full of lies,
My mind's burning.

I smell jealousy's poison,
I'm suffocating in anger's black,
For now, I'm never moving forward,
Just back and back.

Anger's a disease, jealousy a poison,
Both a torture song.
Tears stream down my cheek,
I wish I were gone.

Carys Coleman (10)
St Mark's CE Primary School, Hadlow Down

Anger

Anger sounds like someone playing the violin on a very high note,
Anger's colour is the smoky fire which warms the air,
Anger's animal is an eagle gliding in the air,
Anger's smell is the smell of onions,
Anger feels like a ton of hailstones.

Stefan Godfrey (9)
St Mark's CE Primary School, Hadlow Down

The Ring Of Emotions

That ring Grandma always wears,
It's strange, not normal at all,
It's like a mix of emotions,
Happy, angry, sad and scared.

It booms with emotions as if it's a pot overloaded.

Happy greets you like birds swooping and twittering,
Angriness storms in like the crashing of thunder and lightning,
Sadness overwhelms you until you're on the verge of tears,
Scaredness sends a shiver down your spine and you go cold.

Happiness is like rabbits hopping over the peaceful, green hills,
Angriness is like a bull charging towards you in a field,
Sadness is like a dead bird falling from the sky,
Scaredness is like a mouse running, running, running away.

That ring Grandma always wears - it's strange.

Helen Michaelson-Yeates (9)
St Mark's CE Primary School, Hadlow Down

Poem On Anger

Feels like spiky prickles turning to fire
And burning out of control.
Smells like burning hay
And breathing in thick, black smoke.
Fire burning my mouth like red-hot chillies
Enclosed into a small, hot room.
Like swimming in a pool of lava.
Standing on a boiling, cutting slicer,
Cutting you and burning you,
Hot ashes raining and falling on you.

Declan Dunkley (9)
St Mark's CE Primary School, Hadlow Down

Anger

Anger feels hard, hot and rough
Like a burning brick wall.
It smells of burning rubber
And it tastes of fire.
The sound of screeching brakes
And nails on a blackboard.
Anger is deep red.
It charges like a bull.

Amy-Lee Stiller (9)
St Mark's CE Primary School, Hadlow Down

Love

Love is as soft as a dove's song,
With scented candles wafting lavender.
It feels as if champagne is bubbling inside you.
It sings out to you like a dove.
It looks as pink as a little girl's bedroom.
It tastes as good as butter on a jacket potato.

Tilly Sherwood (10)
St Mark's CE Primary School, Hadlow Down

Anger

Anger
Hot as boiling, red fire
Blasting out of a volcano.
Smells like red-hot burnt skin,
Roars like a black, white and orange tiger.
Feels like a spiky, sharp knife
Burning on your hand.
Tastes like a vat of hot, boiling chillies
Burning on your fork.

Christie McMenamin (10)
St Mark's CE Primary School, Hadlow Down

Anger

It tastes like bitter sand
Going through your mind.
The colour is shiny red
Erupting from a volcano.
It looks like some blood
When somebody has had a fight.
It feels like a hedgehog
Trotting along the road.
Anger is my life today.

Daniel Hansell (8)
St Mark's CE Primary School, Hadlow Down

Anger

Anger sounds like the sun exploding.
Anger feels like a big spike plunging in your hand.
Anger smells like gas trying to pollute your lungs.
Anger looks fiery red.
Anger is like a tiger lashing out for its prey.

Jesse Coleman (8)
St Mark's CE Primary School, Hadlow Down

Happiness

Happiness is a feeling, a feeling of joy.
It tastes like ice cream melting in my mouth.
It smells like burning cinnamon.
It sounds like a soft blue tit singing away.
It feels like a soft, newborn kitten.
Happiness is the colour of yellow, glowing sunshine.
It is a pony cantering down a field.
Happiness is a great feeling.

Claudia Vince (9)
St Mark's CE Primary School, Hadlow Down

Emotions

The sour taste of envy,
The swelling in your throat,
As your friend has everything except happiness,
All the colours of pink, lilac, red and yellow,
The colour of sunshine and friendship,
Lastly anger.
And in your throat, a red, spiky ball,
As you hear a golden flame call.

Elizabeth Durant (10)
St Mark's CE Primary School, Hadlow Down

Blue Is A . . .

Blue is a blob of ink on the page
Blue is a shining drop of water
Blue is a glimmer of the sky through the clouds
Blue is a sight of the sea.

Yellow is a stream of light
Yellow is a beach of sand
Yellow is a trickle of hope
Yellow is a friendship stop.

Orange is a glowing fire
Orange is a good beach ball
Orange is a bad live wire
Orange is a great ball of gas.

Black is the darkness of night
Black is a strange water gutter
Black is a horrid word typed
Black is a dark journey into space.

Green is a happy leaf
Green is a slithering snake
Green is a sour grape
Green is a crazy person's hair.

Alicia White (9)
St Richard's RC School, Chichester

My Sister, Your Sister

My sister's cleverer than your sister,
Yes, my sister's cleverer than yours,
If her brain gets any bigger,
It will burst out of all of the doors!

Yes, but my sister's prettier than your sister,
My sister's prettier, OK?
Others compare her with a rose,
She's even more beautiful I say.

Ah, but my sister's kinder than your sister,
My sister's kinder alright.
If a little kitten was lost in the day,
She would help it, even at night.

Yes, but my sister's better behaved than your sister,
My sister's better behaved than yours.
Her teacher is overwhelmed by the way she behaves,
For she opens and closes all doors!

But my sister doesn't mind your sister,
Mine quite likes yours too.
Perhaps they don't think so much of us!
That might actually be true!

Lucy Brookes (9)
St Richard's RC School, Chichester

Red

Red is a fast, speedy Ferrari car.
Red is a fat, cylindrical postbox with letters bulging out.
Red is Mars spinning in space.
Red is a rose that smells so sweet.
Red is a strawberry bulging in the mouth.
Red is tomato, pips seeping through the lips.

Tom Hurst (9)
St Richard's RC School, Chichester

My House, Your House

My house is bigger than your house.
My house is way bigger than yours.
It is so big you could fit twenty brown bears in it,
But they'd probably rip down the door.

Well, my house is longer than your house.
My house is longer, OK?
It is so long you could fit a train inside it.
Yes, my house is longer in every way.

My house is worth more than your house.
My house is worth many pounds more.
It would take a truckload of money
To buy even a single door.

Well, my house is stronger than your house.
My house is stronger than yours.
It has been hit by ten nuclear bombs
And mauled by giant paws.

Isaac Salt (9)
St Richard's RC School, Chichester

All Together

Athletic Alice ate an awesome apple.
Majestic Matilda munched magical marbles.
Loopy Lucy likes lovely lions.
Jolly Jessica just jumps joyfully.
Luscious Lauren loves licking lemons.
Carefree Caterina catches climbing cats.

Tessa Newman (9)
St Richard's RC School, Chichester

My Mouse, Your Mouse

My mouse is plumper than yours,
He's the one I'm having for tea.
He's so fat he got stuck in his mouse hole
And guess who helped him? Me.

So? My mouse is cleverer than yours,
That means more brains to eat.
I'm saving the brain for dessert
Oh, won't that be a treat!

My mouse is furrier than yours,
He's furrier than King Kong!
And when you decorate trees
You'll get him mixed up with a pompom!

Why can't we just make up?
'Cause I'd love to be your friend.
OK, but on one condition
Your mouse is mine to the end!

Caterina Atkinson (9)
St Richard's RC School, Chichester

About My Friends

Loopy Lucy licks luscious lollies
Awesome Alice ate angry ants
Raging Roisin robs Rebecca
Cool Caterina catches cobwebs
Tiny Tessa tells Tom tall tales
Loud Lauren likes lovely lions.

Melissa Sykes (9)
St Richard's RC School, Chichester

My Brother, Your Brother

My brother's cleverer than your brother,
Yes, my brother's cleverer than yours.
He knows his 225 times table,
In physics he knows all the laws.

Yes, but my brother's kinder than your brother,
My brother's kinder, OK?
He helps set up the table
And his birthday is in May.

Ah, but my brother's better behaved than your brother,
My brother's better behaved alright.
He helps the teacher all day
And helps my mum at night.

Yes, but my brother's more handsome than your brother,
My brother's more handsome I'm sure.
Every time the doorbell rings,
We know it's girls at the door.

Harry Henshaw (9)
St Richard's RC School, Chichester

Blue

Blue is the look of my jeans
Blue is the sight of my front door
Blue is the shirt of my favourite football team
Blue is the cold of the sea
Blue is the wind in the sky
So blue is my favourite colour
And now you know why.

Harry Martin (10)
St Richard's RC School, Chichester

My Cat, Your Cat

My cat's lazier than your cat
My cat's lazier than yours
He sleeps all day upon my bed
Instead of prowling outdoors.

My cat's fatter than your cat
I really don't mean to be rude
He eats three packets of biscuits a day
He's practically bulging with food.

My cat's louder than your cat
My cat's louder, OK?
You can hear him through double glazed windows
You can hear him ten miles away.

My cat's cheekier than your cat
My cat's cheekier I suppose
He answers back to my mum and dad
Then gets a smack on the nose!

My cat rather likes your cat
Mine quite likes yours too
We very rarely know they're there
Supposedly, that's true!

Roisin McNally (10)
St Richard's RC School, Chichester

My Mum (Who's A Bit Dodgy)

My mum (you'll know) is really weird,
She plays the teacups and grows a beard.
One thing about her I especially like
Is her extremely crazy appetite.

She eats baked beans with mouldy fleas,
She eats the beetles that live in the trees.

How she swallows I do not know,
She'd eat Lala, Dipsy and Po
If my little brother didn't love them so.

She won't eat chips or tomato sauce,
Only her usual rotten horse.

The way she consumes is really nutty,
She'd even eat me if I was putty!

The one food that she really craves
Is dictionary pages and mayonnaise.

If she had the chance she'd devour the moon,
Yes, she'd rise in a rocket with a fork and a spoon.

One day though, she gulped down a snake,
But the venom we thought was more than she'd take,

We hired a crane to take the fat body
Straight to hospital, which is always quite dodgy.

We dreamed and we hoped and prayed that she'd live,
The dream came true and she's still eating squid!

Claudia Tyler (10)
St Thomas More's Catholic Primary School, Havant

The Ghosts Of The Fairground

Ancient memories
Glide into her senseless mind,
The fairground,
Is her graveyard,
Wandering through the rides,
She screeches,
Answering screeches follow,
Gliding ghosts emerge on every side,
There is no escape,
Snack hut doors slam,
Cash machines clink,
Music drifts from the carousel
Like a mist,
The spinning cups,
Moan and groan into action,
A black sheet covers the graveyard,
There is no escape.

Aimee Rogers (10)
Southwater Junior School, Horsham

Star

As I glimmer in the black,
As I seek out the house,
Through the mist
I struggle,
To see a rickety stair of
Smashed marble floor,
I long to see more,
I see them sometimes,
I see them all,
With the littered light
I give,
As years pass,
I stay the same,
I still shine in the sky.

Olivia Watkinson (10)
Southwater Junior School, Horsham

The Ghost Of The Underground

He walks through the underground,
Breathing in the smell of minty chewing gum.
Dark as a dungeon
Is the underground,
His home,
Where he died.
His face is wrinkled like a crumpled piece of paper.
The signs are cracked,
Falling down.
He silently tears down the advertisements,
Like a hungry cat.
His gas mask rattles in its box,
Hanging limply from his neck.
He whispers for you . . .
Aching to be alive again.

Louisa Clark (10)
Southwater Junior School, Horsham

Flower

I am weakened,
Disintegrating,
Dying, painstakingly slowly.
I long to see the sun's rays shining,
I shrivel sluggishly - sagging,
Limping like an aged dog.
I am lonely waiting for my fate,
Longing to die,
To leave this godforsaken planet.
Every day when I wake,
I see my dream,
But reality blinds me,
Torture over and over again.

William Nash (10)
Southwater Junior School, Horsham

If I Had Fins

If I had fins
>> I would touch the sandy bottom of the wavy sea and
>> Swoop around the rocks.

If I had fins
>> I would taste the salty water and use shiny shells to
>> Make beautiful necklaces.

If I had fins
>> I would listen to the snapping of sharks and swim
>> Away with the screeching dolphins.

If I had fins
>> I would breathe on the slimy coral
>> And shine it up.

If I had fins
>> I would gaze at the pointy ends of fishing rods and
>> Glide away with the current.

If I had fins
>> I would dream of swimming in a shoal of fish and be
>> Able to see up through the glimmering water.

Anja Dolphin (11)
Southwater Junior School, Horsham

Moonbeam

So straight,
Glimmering.
I move like a cheetah,
I flicker.
Glaring into the darkness,
Winking.
When I light up the night sky,
I dazzle.
I'm as bright as a floodlight,
Blazing.
I brighten the night sky.

Adam Hockley (10)
Southwater Junior School, Horsham

Candlestick

Standing on a marble fireplace
Made of gold with jade
Candle on me
Drip, drip, dripping on my face
It burns, stinging me
Pain surging up
My anger
Ready to erupt
Like a volcano
But my candle is burning
Down, down
Soon the blackness
Will overpower us
But the room
Will always be the same.

Jack Wilcox (11)
Southwater Junior School, Horsham

Tree

So bumpy,
you may call me rough.
You call me
and your hands afterwards
are not smooth anymore.
A cold breeze comes.
I shiver as leaves fall
in front of my face
making a tingle down my spine.
I want to move, to scratch
of course
I cannot
but it is annoying.
I have waited centuries

I need a friend,
someone to swing from my branches.

Charlotte Cowlin (11)
Southwater Junior School, Horsham

The Ghost Of The Attic

I climbed up the stairs
To the attic,
Saw the cobwebs
In the moonlight.
Dust came to my terrified eyes.
The rafters rattled,
The floorboards creaked,
The trapdoor banged.
I smelt the rotting smell.
I went to find my missing toy,
Instead I saw a boy.
A picture moved,
I heard whistling sounds,
Saw a giant spider on the ground.
Suddenly I could taste the danger,
But before I could draw breath,
          I . . . !

Isabelle Allison (10)
Southwater Junior School, Horsham

Ivy

I slither silently
Up the side of the sill
Of a squalid,
Sordid window,
Like a devious fox,
A choker around a neck,
A deceitful snake,
I entwine round life,
A crafty fiend,
Furtive and treacherous,
Come through the gate
Never to return.

Chloe Miles (9)
Southwater Junior School, Horsham

If I Had Fins

If I had fins
    I would touch the soft seabed
        That's at the bottom of the sea.

If I had fins
    I would taste the krill
        As they float like bubbles in the sea.

If I had fins
    I would listen to the current
        That carries me through the ocean.

If I had fins
    I would breathe the ocean's scent
        As I glide through the clear ocean.

If I had fins
    I would gaze at the beautiful fish
        As they glide gracefully through the ocean.

If I had fins
    I would dream of jumping through the water
        And weaving through the slimy seaweed.

Jennifer Powell (10)
Southwater Junior School, Horsham

If I Had Fins

If I had fins, I would touch the slippery surface of seaweed
And get swept away in the southern current.

If I had fins, I would taste the salty water of the deep blue
And swim with a million other fish.

If I had fins, I would listen to the waves crashing on the shore
And dive down to search for more.

If I had fins, I would breathe in the red water of the shark's ex-prey
And dart away just in case.

If I had fins, I would gave a the sun
Gleaming through the surface.

If I had fins, I would dream of having arms
And start it all over again!

Drew Taylor (10)
Southwater Junior School, Horsham

Playtime

Jumping high
Jumping low
To the sky
To the ground
Jumping round and round

Flying through the air
Twirling in the sky
Running round in circles
Skipping back and forth.

Emily Meeks (7)
Tollgate Community Junior School, Eastbourne

Sunset

B last of orange
E very single night
A lways quiet
U nusually graceful
T ime and time again
I t is a magical sight
F ull of colours
U tterly peaceful
L ingering light

S uper feeling
U nbeatably calming
N atural light
S plendid
E xquisite
T ranquil and silent.

Samantha Steer (10)
Tollgate Community Junior School, Eastbourne

Rumble

Thunder boomed from the air
The wind was fighting
A tornado struck and came from nowhere
The sky went dark and it started to get windy
But why?
Was it the last day of Earth
Or did the clouds want revenge
On all the planes passing by?
But still no answer
All you can do is wait!

Bayan Fenwick (10)
Tollgate Community Junior School, Eastbourne

I Saw A Dolphin

I saw a dolphin
        In the sea
                I wonder if
                        It saw me
                                Its eyes
Were shining
        Like the sun
                It was having
                        Lots of fun!
                                It was
Dancing
        On the waves
                It looked very beautiful
                        In the sea.
I hope it saw me.

Ella Garraway (8)
Tollgate Community Junior School, Eastbourne

All About Me

Look at me, I'm as tall as a tree
And happy as can be.

Kind and polite,
My eyes shine bright.

Smart and kind,
I won't leave my friends behind.

My mum said I'm clever,
She'll be my friend forever.

Sweet as a treat,
My writing is always neat.

Bronwyn Ryan (7)
Tollgate Community Junior School, Eastbourne

The Queen's Reply

When I was at the zoo
I met the Queen herself
But strangely, she was on an envelope
I ripped her off and stuck her on the antelope!

She still didn't look quite herself
A bit like a hairy vacuum cleaner
So when we came across the shark, I stuck it on one
And then when I saw her closely
The Queen looked even meaner!

So I ripped and pulled quite hard
And she finally came off the shark
I called out pleasantly
'Thank goodness I saved you,'
But I got no remark.

Dabbing carefully at her head, I was still quite puzzled
Where was the rest of her shoulders and below?
What was the reason for her feet?
Why didn't she have any meat?
Then I realised the Queen was different
So she must have been feeling low.

I gave her to my mum, although she looked annoyed
And I asked her what was the matter
'The postage stamp is what the matter is
For it cost me 25p!'
And then she yelled,
'You're grounded. Oh, and stop the chatter!'

Emily Bailey (10)
Tollgate Community Junior School, Eastbourne

Clouds

The clouds they floated everywhere,
I went away to see the mare,
Then I ate a big, green pear,
A little bee flew on my head
And then I said, 'I'm going to bed.'

When in bed I had a dream,
Of strawberry jelly and ice cream,
So much jelly it made me scream,
Jelly and ice cream in a heap,
What a beautiful way to go to sleep.

I dreamt again of clouds so high,
The clouds were made of apple pie,
They flew with the sun in the sky,
Hundreds and thousands fell like the rain,
I wish I were in my dream again.

When I awoke I was so sad,
There was no jelly to be had,
Just the smiling face of Dad,
Can't wait until tonight,
When I can dream of clouds and sleep real tight.

Amy Garnell (7)
Tollgate Community Junior School, Eastbourne

My Favourite Hobby

T rampolines make you go really high when you jump,
R ight up in the sky,
A ll day long if I could.
M y mum is scared of doing seat drops,
P ipe jumps, straddles and tuck jumps.
O livia is a champion.
L ove bouncing all day.
I love bouncing high with my sister, Jessica.
N o one goes as high as me.
E lephants can't go on it.

Olivia Groves (7)
Tollgate Community Junior School, Eastbourne

Budgies

I have two budgies
They are pretty, but noisy
Their names are Joe and Jo Anne
They are green, blue and yellow
They talk all day to each other
I wish I knew what they were saying
Perhaps they're talking about me.

Laura Cardin (7)
Tollgate Community Junior School, Eastbourne

Feet

F eet are marvellous things
    The things we put in our shoes
E xtremely squishy, very odd
E xtra weird rectangular toes
T he trouble is, they are quite smelly!

Lydia Crossey (8)
Tollgate Community Junior School, Eastbourne

My First Day

I was scared,
Terrified even,
So frightened,
My soul drained out of me,
I was dreading the day,
But after it had finished,
It was OK,
Besides, it was only my first day.

Liam Mason (10)
Tollgate Community Junior School, Eastbourne

Henry The Tudor King

Henry VIII was a Tudor king,
When he was young he learnt to sing.

Henry was so very fat,
His tummy bulged over where he sat.

He was so very overweight,
He was always late to meet a date.

Henry really liked his pies,
But sometimes he told big fat lies.

Henry was so very lazy,
When he got old his eyes got hazy.

Henry had a very big boat,
He liked to sail it round and gloat.

Henry had six wives,
Many of whom lost their lives,
Although I think he preferred his chives.

One of Henry's wives was Anne of Cleves,
When they got divorced she was not pleased.

Rachel Limage (9)
Western Road Community Primary School, Lewes

King Henry VIII

K ing Henry was obese
I n fact he was a beast
N othing would be left in the larder
G reat Scott, he was obese.

H e got a gash that would not heal
E very day it got easier to feel
N o more riding could he do
R edder and redder it grew
Y es, it would not heal.

Beth Arscott (9)
Western Road Community Primary School, Lewes

Rhyming Henry

Henry VIII was so fat he had a semi-circle cut out where he sat.
Henry learnt to play the lute as quick as you would say 'hoot'.
When the bells would ring, young Henry learnt to sing.

When Henry was older he had six wives, which he treated like
a bunch of chives.
He was so overweight and always late.
Although dinner was a different matter, he was always there
eating his batter.

Henry grew ulcers on his legs, he failed to walk and would rarely talk.
Poor Henry, he was so sad to see each empty plate, although it
was nothing compared to his terrible weight.
Even the ablutions, he had to find solutions.
But sadly he died and couldn't eat any more pies.

Tamara Carruthers-Cole (9)
Western Road Community Primary School, Lewes

King Henry VIII

King Henry VIII was so fat
If he sat on a cat
He would squash it flat.

He hated France
And loved to joust
With a lance.

He was also tall
And loved to dance
At a ball.

Henry VIII couldn't walk
So instead
He ate roast pork.

Will Anthony (9)
Western Road Community Primary School, Lewes

Henry VIII

Henry couldn't walk because he ate too much pork.
Henry was a Tudor king and he liked to dance and sing.

Henry was young and such a thrill,
But when he grew up, he planned to kill.

Henry wanted to declare war on France,
But, he never gave the French a chance.

Yoli Ward-Streeter (9)
Western Road Community Primary School, Lewes

Henry VIII

Henry VIII was so fat,
He could squash a cat.
Henry VIII had over 100 instruments.
Henry VIII loved to dance,
Henry VIII hated France.
Henry VIII was so tall,
He was bigger than some walls.

JJ Frizell (9)
Western Road Community Primary School, Lewes

Henry VIII

Henry VIII was so fat,
He could squash a cat.
Henry led the army to war
And his army wasn't poor.

Ayisha Ascioglu (9)
Western Road Community Primary School, Lewes

Henry VIII

He was fat, he was overweight,
Yes, you guessed it, it's Henry VIII.
Henry played jousting with two poles called lances,
He also did lots of dances.
Henry was a Tudor king,
He like to dance, hunt and sing.
Henry had six wives, I will tell you three,
Catherine of Aragon, Catherine Howard and Catherine Parr.
All these Catherines came from near and far.
Henry had a bad temper,
You wouldn't want to play with him.
He would chop your head off,
Oh, what a mean king.

Beth Crouch (9)
Western Road Community Primary School, Lewes

Henry VIII

Henry VIII
Was very overweight.

He was very bright,
But not very light.

He did not do his ablutions,
So he had to find solutions.

He loved to play the lute
And he loved to play the flute.

He fell in love with Anne Boleyn,
Which the Roman Pope thought was a sin.

Louise Astbury (9)
Western Road Community Primary School, Lewes

Henry VIII

Henry was a powerful king,
He liked to dance and sing.

Henry was a very fat king,
He married six times and one was Anne Boleyn.

Her head was cut off, so that was the end of Anne Boleyn,
She died because she couldn't give a son to him.

The other ones died or were divorced after a few years,
He never shed any tears.

By then Henry was very fat,
He died from ulcers, so that was the end of that.

Alice Chapman (9)
Western Road Community Primary School, Lewes

Henry VIII

Henry VIII was great
And had six dates in the British states.
He was so fat,
He could flatten a cat.
Henry VIII was a Tudor king,
He liked to dance and sing.
Henry was as fat as two pigs,
He would eat a million figs.
He wasn't left alone,
He could eat a chicken to the bone.

Luke Tomsett (9)
Western Road Community Primary School, Lewes

Henry VIII

There was a king who was very fat,
Yes, he was Henry VIII, old chap.
He did jousting with a lance in his hand
And always did it in his own land.
He was too fat,
They cut a semi-circle out of the place he sat.
From when Henry was king he didn't do his ablutions,
But he came up with some good solutions.
But as Henry got older he could not walk,
Was it because he ate too much pork?
No, he had an achy leg
And for breakfast he sometimes had egg.

Xanthe Wharton (9)
Western Road Community Primary School, Lewes

Henry VIII Poem

Henry was as fat as a moose,
He was so large, his belts were loose,
The reason for this was that he ate too much goose.
He had six wives,
Two beheaded, one died, two divorced
And one survived.
He got the son he always wanted,
His name was Edward.
He became King, just like his father,
But he would much rather . . .
Be less fat!

Kaleem Luthra (9)
Western Road Community Primary School, Lewes

King Henry VIII

Henry was so very fat,
They cut a semi-circle where he sat.
He was so very overweight,
He could not go to visit his date.
But when he ate,
He ate like a saint
And he munched
And he crunched
And he ate quite a bunch.
As Henry grew older,
He could not walk,
In fact he was so fat,
He could snap a fork.

Noah Preston (10)
Western Road Community Primary School, Lewes

Henry VIII

The bell rings, ding, ding, ding, ding!
Hey look, here comes the king, the king!
I think I know a bit about him.

Henry VIII was extremely fat,
He had a half circle cut out where he sat.
This lazy king had liked to gloat,
Over his lovely, charming boat.

Henry VIII had a lute
And on his trumpet he went *toot, toot!*
One of his servants, the Groom of the Stool,
Would wash him and bathe him in a great pool.

Megan Edwards (9)
Western Road Community Primary School, Lewes

Leon The Lion

I once knew a lion called Leon,
He always sat on a log,
He'd jump through a hoop or fetch a stick,
He was rather like a dog.

I once knew a tiger called Timmy
And he always sat in a tree,
He'd sit up there all day long
And once made friends with a flea.

I once knew an otter called Otto
And he always hid in a hole,
He'd hide there for an hour or so
And once saw a cute little mole.

I once knew an eagle called Eddie
And he always ate dead mice,
And this massive animal was quite like himself
And I found him rather nice.

Zoë Vernon (8)
Western Road Community Primary School, Lewes

Henry VIII

Henry VIII was married six times,
I wonder why.
Henry VIII was so immature
And he led his army to war.
Henry VIII was as big as an ape
And he always ate, ate, ate.
Henry was so plump, not little,
And he played the fiddle.

Laura Keenan-Hall (9)
Western Road Community Primary School, Lewes

Silence

Silence is white,
Like a soft duvet made of clouds,
Covering a white marshmallow bed.

It sounds like something drifting, floating
And then falling slowly to Earth,
As the silence is broken
By the answer to whatever caused this pause.

It sometimes smells like nothing in particular,
But if you are lucky,
It smells like a place where everyone goes only once.

It tastes like feathers
And places where nobody has ever been,
Or ever will go.

It feels like a soft pillow,
But at the same time, it feels like something new
That only you know about and is special.

It looks like something very warm and fluffy,
But also it looks sharp and brittle,
Like it could snap at any moment.

It reminds me of the first snowfall of winter,
When you are the first person to go outside in the cold and white,
While all around you is . . .
Silence.

Bryony Hockin (10)
Western Road Community Primary School, Lewes

Anger

Anger is black like a tiger's stripes.
Anger smells like something burning.
Anger tastes like courgettes and red-hot chilli peppers.
Anger looks like the sky at night.
Anger feels like having your heart broken.
Anger sounds like a lion roaring.

Madeleine Lewis (10)
Western Road Community Primary School, Lewes

Silence

Silence smells of everything.
It reminds of the far-off times.
It feels like peace.
It sounds like peace.
It looks like a wreath of everlasting stillness.
It tastes like warm apple pie.
Silence is blue like the sky.
Silence is blue like the sky.

Jack Arscott (11)
Western Road Community Primary School, Lewes

Lewes Castle

Go to the top of Lewes Castle
And what can you see?
I can see an army approaching
And they are coming closer
And their triggers are up
And that one is saying, 'Hands up,'
And the soldiers put their hands up
And the soldiers say, 'If you fight we will kill you
And you will die.'

Eddie Lansley (7)
Western Road Community Primary School, Lewes

Henry VIII

Henry VIII could squash a cat flat as a mat.
Some he would behead and others would dread.
A milk jug he might smash, but he wouldn't take out the trash.
He had lots of cash and he got fat as quick as a flash.
He was fatter than a tree and more famous than me.
He was too old for toys, but he couldn't hang out with the boys.
He had six wives, but he wasn't a cat with nine lives.

Rupert Flowers (9)
Western Road Community Primary School, Lewes

Love

Love is white like a light in a darkened room,
It tastes like strawberries on a summer's afternoon.
It smells like a rose, spattered with rain,
It feels like the smoothness of a horse's mane.
It looks like a heart on a cloud of air,
It sounds like the laughter at a village fair.
It reminds me of laughter and happiness,
And fun, and . . . !

Love is gold like the ring on your finger,
It feels like something that exists to linger.
It tastes like chocolate, all over your face,
It smells like mowed grass, all over the place!
It looks like a parcel all wrapped up with paper,
It sounds like the sewing of a hard-working draper.
It reminds me of laughter, and happiness,
And fun, and . . . !
Well, love reminds me of *you.*

Vita Bowman (10)
Western Road Community Primary School, Lewes

Fear

Fear is transparent like water
Fear looks like a ball of mystery
Fear smells like burning petrol
Fear sounds like a high-pitched note
Fear feels breathtaking
Fear tastes like lemons
Fear reminds me of tingling toes
Fear is in the air now
Fear! Fear! Fear! Fear! Fear!

Rosie Chapman (10)
Western Road Community Primary School, Lewes

King Henry VIII

King, King, King Henry VIII,
He always fought the present wars
And he tried not to break the laws.

King, King, King Henry VIII,
Oh, how he loved Anne Boleyn,
He wanted Catherine of Aragon to sin.

King, King, King Henry VIII,
Oh, how he ate, oh how he ate,
He had a lot to date.

King, King, King Henry VIII.

Thomas Morrish (10)
Western Road Community Primary School, Lewes

Henry VIII

Henry VIII hated France,
But he loved to dance.

He was very bright,
But not very light.

The Pope wasn't happy when he divorced Catherine
And most people thought it was a sin.

On his flute and his lute,
He liked to have a toot.

Nikolas Long (10)
Western Road Community Primary School, Lewes

Fire

Red eyes burning,
Rage, anger and fury,
Growing like a
Raging hurricane.
Scarlet claws grasp
All in sight.
Barging past helpless,
Defenceless forest.
Spreading like vast wind
Across rough seas,
Destroying all in its path.
Torturing and terrorising,
Ripping grass,
Staining it with ash,
Spitting, burning
Poison.
Then disappears,
Leaving terrified victims
Behind.

Isabel Lloyd (10)
Winton Primary School, Bournemouth

Fog

Skinny old man, slinking
Through London streets.
His long raincoat and hat hides
Him from the modern world.
Sneaking through houses in dark corners,
Reaching out with bony fingers to
Steal.
Crouching, hiding as he glides past houses,
Mice and rats eat at him as
He shuffles past,
His dirty beard dragging along
The alleyway floor.

Andrew Lavender (11)
Winton Primary School, Bournemouth

Fire

Reaching for trees,
Grabbing them,
For a feed.

After they're
Gobbled,
It's down,
Ready to pounce
On victims.

Roaring,
Over the vast forest trees,
Helpless.
Ready to be struck
By the heat.

Can knock trees over
At great heights.
The fire multiplying,
Trees helping.

Emily Riddiough (10)
Winton Primary School, Bournemouth

Fire

His scarlet clothes
Were flowing,
As he fiercely pushed
Through the helpless forest,
Sniffing out fear on the way.
His evil eyes gleamed
Before touching his prey
With sizzling claws.
As soon as he covered his victim
With his ruby cloak,
He sang his gentle song.

Valerija Lvova (10)
Winton Primary School, Bournemouth

Fire!

Destroying
Helpless victims with his orange claws,
Barging past
Helpless branches and trees,
His ruby coat
Covers his prey with spices dripping,
His lethal punch
Destroys many victims' lives.
His angry eyes
Scare victims and they drop candles
And make him huge
And . . . *die!*
Spider-shaped claws
Strangle his enemies,
He is very stealthy
As he tries finding food.

Daniel Burden (10)
Winton Primary School, Bournemouth

Fire Poem

He destroyed helpless trees
Falling apart as he passed by,
Scarlet spices dripped from his
Amber fingertips.
His gold, destructive fists
Punched the defenceless door down.
His burning mouth cracked, spat
And roared with anger in his voice.
Razor-tongue, slicing, dagger-teeth
Ripping victim,
Dark red claws tearing open
The innocent target.
Creeping with noiseless steps,
Gliding through the hallway.

Jade Atkinson & Tayler Smith (10)
Winton Primary School, Bournemouth

Fire

Amber claws creeping
Across scorched grass.
Slowly, cautiously advancing
On helpless victim.
White-hot sparks exploding
All around,
As burning flames meet smooth timber.
Carries on, hunting down
More unsuspecting prey.
Smells fear, burns with even more
Roaring rage.
Ruby eyes scanning, scarlet talons growing,
Swaying, war dance, to and fro.
Then, splash, soak, crackles, retreats,
Then gone,
With a blink of an eye.

Tegen Jones (11)
Winton Primary School, Bournemouth

Fire

Ripping helpless forest apart
With tangy, ruby claws.

Evil lurking in eyes,
Showing he's angry.

Flames spat out remains of wood,
Scarlet spices laughing.

As amber body glowing
In light of full moon.

Fern Whiting (10)
Winton Primary School, Bournemouth

Fog

He crouched down,
To slip past
The haunted alleyways,
Thin, but vast.

Hovered above streets,
At a very tired rate,
With a ripped, dull shirt,
An old, scruffy state.

Small tears froze,
Before they hit the ground,
From his loneliness and hunger,
The freezing man frowned.

His scruffy little terrier,
Following behind,
To help him along,
Poor and blind.

He avoided lamp posts,
Lanterns, any light,
So he wouldn't be seen,
On this late, misty night.

Lisa Mills (10)
Winton Primary School, Bournemouth

Sunshine

Heat,
From the flaming sun.
Its rays of sunshine,
Take control of the people.
Works,
Hours shining over the different countries.
The heat,
As hot as an oven.
It wanders the sky
With its power to move itself.
When it's early,
The sun will rise,
When it's late the sun will fade.
Its brightness,
Its light,
Even sometimes its kindness,
But maybe its *anger*
Will give you a bit of a scare.
You will see it shake, like a heap of rocks falling down a cliff.
The light,
As beautiful as a field full of flowers.

Georgia Wallen (10)
Winton Primary School, Bournemouth

Fire

He hovers
  Over victims
    Waiting to
      Pounce.
        Punching with
          Desert-hot
          Fists,
            He shatters
            Rock with
              One blow.
                Indian spices
                  Sizzling your
                    Nose.
                      Reaching for
                        Weak, helpless
                          Prey.
                            He's the fire,
                              Watch out
                                For his
                                  Stealthy mind.

Charles Rodriguez (10)
Winton Primary School, Bournemouth

Fog

Moody, distressed,
For being stuck in the past.
Yellow teeth gleamed,
He struggled on.
Scruffy long hair,
Clumps of mud,
Swayed in the late evening light.
Thick sticky taped glasses,
Loomed over his face.
He struggled along.
A brown matted dog followed,
Sneakily,
Old baggy trousers,
Ripped grey shirt,
Dangled down.
His slippers were wearing through,
He slid along,
The old man walked on through,
Paths of London.
He also carried all he owned.

Rachel Drewitt (11)
Winton Primary School, Bournemouth

Fire

He swiftly moved through forest,
Scarlet spices drip,
Drip,
Dripping,
From his ruby-red cloak.
His prey's footsteps were getting
Closer.

His victim's heart was pounding in
His ear,
Like a parade of drums getting
Further,
And further,
And further
Down the road.
Roaring at the harmless houses,
Breaking all the windows,
Running and screaming,
Was all the noise that could be
Heard in the death trap.

Emily Head (10)
Winton Primary School, Bournemouth

Night Fire

Fire creeps and crawls
And stalks its prey,
Then it hunts and destroys
Them all.

Ruby cloak,
Those glowing eyes,
Black smoke drifts,
For all to smell.

The night fires,
Growling,
Rumbling grounds,
Making trees tremble all around.

Sparkling flames,
Sizzling grass,
Helpless victim,
Standing by.
Will you be next?

Simon Barton (10)
Winton Primary School, Bournemouth

Fire

Yellow
Angry
Eyes
Hunt for
Me.

Red, orange and
Yellow sparks
Fly.
They're getting closer.

Charges through helpless
Forest.
Orange claws
Reach out!

Ruby coat
Covers fear-filled
Prey!

The flames cracked,
Roared
And scratched
With anger.

Scarlet spices
Dripping
From his red,
Yellow, orange,
Body!

Beth Lamb (10)
Winton Primary School, Bournemouth

Fire

Sapphire,
Shaded nose,
Smells fear.
Crawling around
Doubling,
Near prey.
Approaches
With caution,
Surrounding victims.
Masala cloak
Dripping,
Scarlet spices.
Exploding fist
Burning
The air.
Ripping
Trees bare,
With burning
Claws.
He's stealthy,
Charging
Through forest
Burning.

Jacob West (11)
Winton Primary School, Bournemouth

The Vacuum Monster

It sucks up
The mess on the floor,
It turns and
Mumbles,
Munching objects in its
Way.
Its slate body
With its long,
Windy
Tail dragging behind,
Its lit-up eye
Cyclops-like,
With its whirlwind
Insides,
Breathes
Out fumes,
Stealthily watching
Your every move.

Mica Cornell (10)
Winton Primary School, Bournemouth

Fire

Approaches with
Caution
Ruby coat
Melts with fear
Down to roots of trees.
Screams!
Barges past
Helpless trees.
Manages to
Destroy
Pleading branches.
Masala breath throws
Sparks.
He ran away
With fear.
Dies down
    Down
        Down
            Down.

Nadia Ghazal (10)
Winton Primary School, Bournemouth

Fire

Blue tints
Cover
His spiky hair.
Yellow
Flaming eyes
Stalking
His prey.
Razor
Teeth ripping the branches leaving the tree
Bare.
His roar
Shook
The ground.
Spices dripping from his amber cloak.
Stalking
Behind his victim then
Pouncing!

Charlotte Caesar (10)
Winton Primary School, Bournemouth

My Dog, Alfie

My dog is fat
He wears a big red hat.
He chases the cat
On the mat.

He is white
And he can fly a kite.
He is small
And he plays with a ball.

He is funny
And he wees on the bunny.
His name is Alfie
And he is mouthy.

Nathan James (10)
Wyke Regis Junior School, Weymouth

The Weird United

I was playing football tomorrow.
I scored a hat-trick like Rooney Wayne.
Rooney Wayne plays golf on a football pitch
And football on a golf course.
Rooney Wayne told a mate that he scored 64 under par on a
football pitch.
Ronaldo Cristiano scored even though he did not play.
Giggs Ryan scored an own goal deliberately.
Ferdinand Rio had a bath and shower on a cricket pitch.
O'Shea John ran into the linesman and knocked him out.
Keane Roy got sent off for a yellow card.
Neville Gary hit the ref around the head with a tennis ball.
Nistelrooy Van Ruud scored a good goal but it was rubbish.
Silvestre Mikel scored from the crowd.
Ferguson Alex Sir tripped over his own feet.
Howard Tim made a superb save but did not.
Bellion David passed to the wrong team.
A good day for United, they lost 8-1 in the end.

Joe Allen (10)
Wyke Regis Junior School, Weymouth

What Did Life Feel Like To Be An Evacuee?

E motional
V agrant
A ccused
C hildren
U seless
A lone
T errified
I nvolved
O bligation
N ervous.

The Second World War began September 1st, 1939.
War starts, evacuation begins.

Sophie King (11)
Wyke Regis Junior School, Weymouth

Where Am I?

My shape is weird
My shape is fun
If I get away
I'll be on the run.

My shape is long
My shape is short
I could be
In the tennis court.

My shape is fat
My shape is thin
I could be in the hairdressers
Getting a trim.

My shape is big
My shape is small
I could be
In Istanbul.

My shape is cool
My shape is normal
I will be
In the swimming pool.

Edward Beauchamp (10)
Wyke Regis Junior School, Weymouth

Arsenal

Thierry Henry, Jose Antonio Reyes and Pires
Are the top scorers in this team.
Football, football is so great
When you score, we celebrate.
Arsenal, Arsenal, you're the best
When we win we show the rest
That we are the best!

George Dukes (10)
Wyke Regis Junior School, Weymouth

My Friend, Jimmy!

Hi, my name is Josh
Yes, I know it sounds posh.
But I'm just a normal bloke
And I love to drink Coke.

I have a friend who likes to drive me round the bend
His name is Jimmy and he drives a Mini.
He has a pet piranha
And he feeds it big bananas.

He often shops at Asda, where he usually buys lots of plasters
He gets bitten by his piranha because it thinks his finger is a banana.
He also has a cat, but his cat is a bit fat.
His name is Sam and he supports West Ham.
Jimmy likes counting money, but he hates eating honey.
He is a very strange mate,
But he really is *great!*

Joshua Jenkins (10)
Wyke Regis Junior School, Weymouth

Andy

There was a man called Andy,
Who loved eating candy.

This man called Andy,
Married Miss Mandy.

This Miss Mandy,
Ate all the candy.

After a week Andy,
Missed his candy.

Then Miss Mandy,
Bought more candy.

And Andy and Mandy,
Lived like a dandy.

David Bain (10)
Wyke Regis Junior School, Weymouth

My Pet Pig

I have a pet pig,
That wears a hairy wig.

She rolls in the mud
And hits the ground with a thud.

She plays with the bunny
And I think it's very funny.

My bunny hides under the shed
And makes himself a cosy bed.

Stella squeals when she's hungry,
She squeals when she's sad,

She squeals late at night,
The only time she stops is when it's very light,

Unless she is hungry in the morning,

She will squeal, squeal, squeal,
If she is not fed in time.

Mica Satchell (10)
Wyke Regis Junior School, Weymouth

Is This Your Head?

My mother said to get ahead,
I don't think this one's mine,
I found it on the flowers,
Beside the table made of pine.
Yesterday I learnt to fly
And landed on cloud nine.
When I find it,
Be sure to come and dine.
Before all this happened,
I was completely fine.

Robyn Nixon (10)
Wyke Regis Junior School, Weymouth

Weird Animals!

Where there are places, there are some faces,
Where there are animals, there are carnivores.

But in the jungle
There is a rumble.

There was a gorilla
As big as Godzilla.

And there are chimps
And they are wimps.

And they were scared
Because they heard

Of Mr Snake,
His name was Jake.

He had a friend, it was a lizard,
That lived in a blizzard.

James Pearson (10)
Wyke Regis Junior School, Weymouth

Fat Cat

I have a fat cat,
Who is lying on a doormat.

When he goes out he gets chased by a dog,
When he comes in he's covered in bog.

When he was a kitten,
He lived in a mitten.

He has been bitten,
By a very big kitten.

He went out and got run over by a car
And he ended up behind a burger bar.
He keeps it a secret.

And he loved it so much,
He is very Dutch.

Megan Arnold (10)
Wyke Regis Junior School, Weymouth

My Poem

M anchester United are the best
A lways put to the test
N eville brothers are so great
C ristiano Ronaldo would be my ideal date
H ow do they do it? No one can see
E nglish champions eight times are we
S cored the triple, never been done
T here are many stories that've been in The Sun
E very time they hit to score
R ed and black is their kit

U nited we stand together
N ever failing, even in bad weather
I n our fans we hope they don't frown
T he Old Trafford is our hometown
E very trophy makes us proud
D eepest thanks to the crowd.

Stacey Bray (10)
Wyke Regis Junior School, Weymouth

My Name

My first is a C, as clever can be,
My second is H, in sweet harmony,
My third is R, respectful by far,
My next is an I,
Followed by S, sometimes shy,
My sixth is a T, once got stung by a bee,
My seventh is an O, overexcited about DT,
My eighth is P, playing my PS2,
My ninth is H, helping people is what I do,
My next is an E, eating sweets from a jar,
My last is an R, I can't wait to drive a car!

Christopher Griffiths (10)
Wyke Regis Junior School, Weymouth

Ghosts

Scary, haunting, little things
Making you scream
With a big, scary beam

That's ghosts

They squiggle down the drain pipe
They walk through the walls
They sneak through the kitchen
They frighten us all

That's ghosts

They cuddle you at night
And tell you it's alright
They're across the hall
If the ghosts decide to have a ball

That's parents!

Louise Daynes (10)
Wyke Regis Junior School, Weymouth

Astronaut

There was a baby, very short,
Who wanted to be an astronaut.
He watched a programme about a man called Neil,
That made him think, *big deal.*
He said to himself, *I can do that,*
Twice as fast because I'm not fat.
He loved the astronauts' suits,
As well as the astronauts' boots.
When he was ten and went to school,
He was only three feet tall.
When he was old, his little theme,
Did not become a dream.

Andrew Whyte (10)
Wyke Regis Junior School, Weymouth

Dream

Have you ever had a dream,
That you know will never come true,
Because it's almost impossible?

      I have.

Have you ever had a dream,
That you've wanted so badly,
You've almost started crying?

      I have.

Have you ever had a dream,
You've always wanted so much to happen,
That you can never stop talking about it?

      I have.

Have you ever had a dream,
That you've always wanted,
You would shake at the thought of it?

      I have.

Evan Feltham (10)
Wyke Regis Junior School, Weymouth

Sunshine

S is for sparkling on the water, setting the scene
U is for universe, that's where the sun is from
N is for never-ending until the world has gone
S is for showing people how important it is
H is for here and not going away
I is for in all of time it has always been here
N is for number of faces that shine when the sun does too
E is for ending of the sun, meaning ending of us.

Sophie Hardy (10)
Wyke Regis Junior School, Weymouth

My Lizard Called Blizzard

Once I had a lizard
And his name was Blizzard.
He liked to explore
And crawled up my door.
He went up a tree,
Then ate a bee.
It gave him a sting,
My, it's a big thing!
Then I said,
'Go to bed.
Next time eat a fly
And you might not die.'
I liked my lizard,
My lizard called Blizzard.

Aarynn Carter (10)
Wyke Regis Junior School, Weymouth

Rainbow

Rainbows are full of imagination,
The colours make your mind wonder about,
They bring smiles to everyone,
No one would dare argue, I doubt.
Rainbows are fascinating
Because the ends disappear,
But it makes them look
Further away than near.
It's their multicolours that dazzle me!

Amber Downing (10)
Wyke Regis Junior School, Weymouth

The Underwater World

There was a shark,
In the dark,
Leaving a red mark.

There were fishes,
Lying on dishes,
There were also fish swimming left, right, up and down,
Making a loud bobbing sound.

At the bottom of the sea,
Octopuses drink some tea,
Did you know there is enough for you and me?

Most of the lochs,
Are made of big rocks,
All the plants,
Make good underpants.

Six dolphins swimming together,
Hopefully forever,
Two sea turtles that are chattery,
Live happily.

Scuba-divers are on their way,
Oh yes, it's the middle of May,
'Look at them,' a scuba-diver said,
'What type of fish is that?' shouted scuba-diver Ted.

The sun is setting,
The fish are avoiding the netting,
All creatures are settling down,
Not a murmur or a sound is around.

Gemma McNie (11)
Wyke Regis Junior School, Weymouth